PHOTO-INSPIRED **ART** QUILTS

CINCINNATI, OHIO
mycraftivity.com
connect. create. explore.

RUFFLED FEATHERS 31" × 26½"

PHOTO-INSPIRED
ART QUILTS

From Composition to Finished Piece

Leni Levenson Wiener

Other fine Krause Publications titles are available from
your local bookstore, craft supply store, online retailer
or visit our website at **www.fwmedia.com**.

13   12   11   10   09   5   4   3   2   1

DISTRIBUTED IN CANADA BY FRASER DIRECT
100 Armstrong Avenue
Georgetown, ON, Canada L7G 5S4
Tel: (905) 877-4411

DISTRIBUTED IN THE U.K. AND EUROPE BY DAVID & CHARLES
Brunel House, Newton Abbot, Devon, TQ12 4PU, England
Tel: (+44) 1626 323200, Fax: (+44) 1626 323319
Email: postmaster@davidandcharles.co.uk

DISTRIBUTED IN AUSTRALIA BY CAPRICORN LINK
P.O. Box 704, S. Windsor NSW, 2756 Australia
Tel: (02) 4577-3555

Library of Congress Cataloging in Publication Data
Wiener, Leni Levenson.
  Photo-inspired art quilts : from composition to finished piece / Leni Levenson
Wiener with Nancy Zieman.
    p. cm.
  ISBN 978-0-89689-804-2 (pbk. : alk. paper)
  1. Embroidery, Machine--Patterns. 2. Photography. 3. Art quilts. I. Zieman,
Nancy Luedtke. II. Title.
  TT772.W537 2009
  746.44'041--dc22
                    2009003094

EDITED BY **VANESSA LYMAN**
INTERIOR DESIGNED BY **JENNIFER HOFFMAN**
COVER DESIGNED BY **NICOLE ARMSTRONG**
PRODUCTION COORDINATED BY **MATT WAGNER**
PHOTOGRAPHY BY **TIM GRONDIN**

Acknowledgments

I would like to thank the following people for their
support and assistance:

- My family—my sons: Jordan, for his artistic advice (and
  his uncanny ability to name an art quilt), and Jared, for
  all his technical assistance; and my husband Fred for
  putting up with the day-to-day disruptions.
- My Art Quilt Monday students for helping me fine-tune
  the techniques in this book.
- At Krause/F+W: Vanessa Lyman for her insight and
  vision in editing this book; Tim Grondin for his photography; Jennifer Hoffman for putting it all into such a
  beautiful package.
- Nancy Zieman and Deanna Springer for getting me
  through all the details of making the DVD—and
  making it fun, besides.

And the following companies for providing materials for
the production of this book:

- Martingale & Company: the Ruby Beholder
- Stretch and Sew, Inc.: Do-Sew
- Blank Quilting, P&B Textiles, FreeSpirit Fabric and
  Robert Kaufman Fabrics for their generosity in provid-
  ing many of the fabrics used in the project quilts and
  other samples in this book.

Metric Conversion Chart

TO CONVERT	TO	MULTIPLY BY
Inches	Centimeters	2.54
Centimeters	Inches	0.4
Feet	Centimeters	30.5
Centimeters	Feet	0.03
Yards	Meters	0.9
Meters	Yards	1.1

An Outstretched Hand   21½" x 30"

TABLE OF **CONTENTS**

WHAT IS AN ART QUILT?   8
HOW TO USE THIS BOOK   10
WHAT YOU WILL NEED   12
BUILDING AN ART QUILT STASH   14
A DESIGN WALL   16
    EXERCISE ONE: *Easy Design Wall*   17

Chapter One
THE ELEMENTS OF GOOD DESIGN   18

Choosing the Subject and Telling A Story   20
Dividing the Composition   21
Choosing the Right Format: Horizontal Versus Vertical   22
Using Lines: Horizontal, Vertical, Diagonal or Curved   23
Taking Better Snapshots   24
Cropping Close for Impact   25
Perspective   26
Leading the Eye In   27
Working With Odd Numbers   28
Placing the Visual Weight   29
Depicting Light and Shadow   30
Understanding Color   32

Chapter Two
FROM PHOTO TO PATTERN   34

Combining Photos for Better Composition   36
EXERCISE TWO: *Combining Photos*   38
EXERCISE THREE: *Cropping*   40
Size Matters   42
Using Photoediting Filters to Create a Pattern   44
EXERCISE FOUR: *Creating A Pattern Without a Computer*   46

Chapter Three
BUILDING A FABRIC COLLAGE   48

Choosing Fabrics for Your Art Quilt   50
EXERCISE FIVE: *Understanding Value*   52
Cutting Your Fabric Pieces   54
EXERCISE SIX: *Tracing Paper or Freezer Paper*   55
Attaching Your Fabric Pieces   56
EXERCISE SEVEN: *Working With Fusible Web*   57
EXERCISE EIGHT: *Creating Your Collage One Element at a Time*   58
EXERCISE NINE: *Choosing a Background Color*   62
EXERCISE TEN: *Deciding on a Composition*   64
Analyzing the Composition   65
EXERCISE ELEVEN: *Building More Complex Art Quilts*   66

Chapter Four
SEWING IT ALL TOGETHER 68

Sewing the Collage in Place 70
Selecting Threads for Thread Painting 71
Free-Motion Stitching 72
EXERCISE TWELVE: *Practicing Free-Motion Stitching* 73
Thread-Painted Accents 74
EXERCISE THIRTEEN: *Direct Thread Painting* 76
EXERCISE FOURTEEN: *Thread-Painted Appliqué* 78
Adding Borders to Your Art Quilt 80
EXERCISE FIFTEEN: *Adding a Border and Border Batting* 82
Adding the Backing 84
Edge Finishes for Your Quilt 85
EXERCISE SIXTEEN: *Making A Binding Edge* 86
EXERCISE SEVENTEEN: *Creating a Pillowcase Edge* 88
EXERCISE EIGHTEEN: *Finishing a Free-Form Shape* 89
Moving Beyond the Frame 90
EXERCISE NINETEEN: *Working Outside of the Box* 91

Chapter Five
CREATIVE ADVICE 92

Naming Your Art Quilt 94
Working In a Series 96
Finding Your Own Voice 97
Artist's Shorthands: Faces 98
Artist's Shorthands: Landscapes 100

Chapter Six
PATTERNS AND PROJECTS 102

Blue Bottle 104
Pansy 106
Autumn 108
Portrait 110
Flamingos 112
Seascape 114
Colonnade 116
Trees in a Grove 118
Tulips 120
Lawn Chairs 122

ABOUT THE AUTHOR 124
RESOURCES 125
INDEX 126

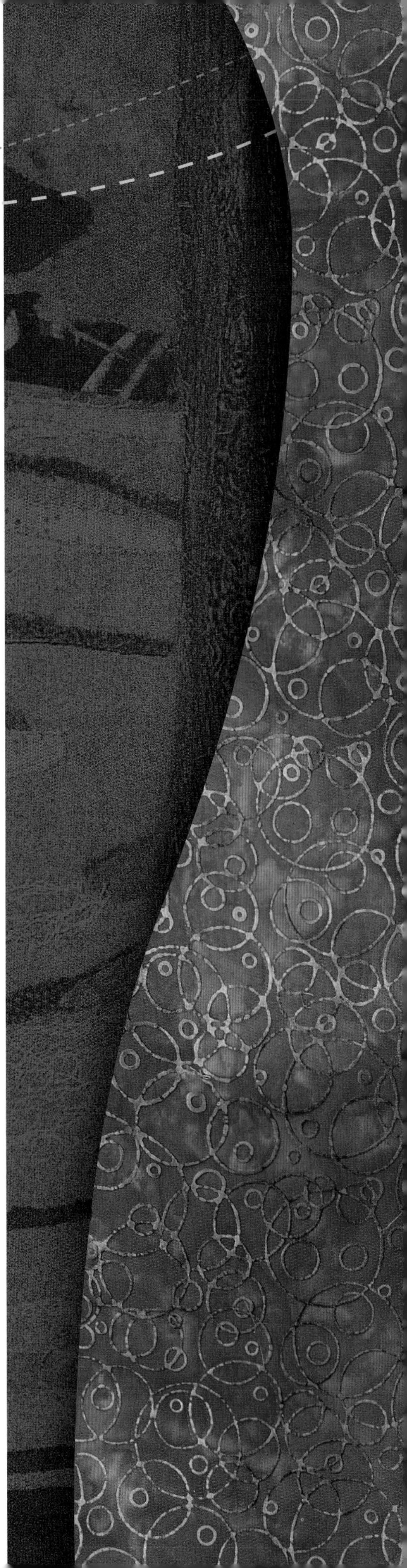

MUSEUM STEPS   21¼" x 30¼"

WHAT IS AN ART QUILT?

Simply put, an art quilt is a work of art, but like a traditional quilt, it is made of fabric (or often fabric and other materials). To be called an art quilt, it must have a top, batting and a bottom layer, and be held together with quilt stitching. Many of the same skills and techniques used for generations to make traditional bed quilts are employed by quilt artists. But these are not quilts to be used on a bed; they are artwork to hang on a wall.

Art quilts have been around for decades, but the trend continues to gain popularity among artists and quilters. Tired of the same sorts of patterns, or of making bed coverings, quilters are looking for new ways to express themselves while still using the same tools and techniques they have learned throughout their traditional quilting years. There are no rules governing how an art quilt is made or what materials it can contain. The art quilt movement has been growing in recent years, with art quilters employing as many ways of creating a work of art as there are artists themselves. There are many ways to create art quilts—piecing, painting, dying, stitching, stamping, beading, weaving, to name just a few, and any combination of these. Since art never goes out of style, neither do art quilts, and making one of these unique and wonderful works of art will open a whole new world for quilters who long to express themselves artistically.

My first book, *Thread Painting* (2007), concentrates on the technique of thread painting, and the projects in the book cover a wide range of interests—quilting, garment sewing, home decor and crafts. My own work in art quilts utilizes the same thread painting technique taught in the book, but in a different environment—the art quilt. An art quilt is a unique and original work of art done in fabric, layered with batting and backed, just like a traditional quilt. Most often, they are made to hang on a wall. Over the past few years, my work has developed and gained acceptance into many art quilt juried shows and venues across the country. My personal style, my voice, is a combination of raw-edge, machine-appliquéed fabric collage with thread painted accents.

Photo-Inspired Art Quilts: From Composition to Finished Piece will start with the basics: what makes an art quilt, how to choose a design, fabric, the importance of color and value, and construction methods. It is more like an art instruction book than a traditional quilt book, and it will allow you to copy some simple examples and then to use your new skills and imagination to move into the world of the art quilt on your own.

This book will illustrate my technique, which is raw-edge machine appliqué with thread painting. I start with a photo as a working guide, which means my art quilts are more representational than abstract. This is by no means the only way to create an art quilt; there are as many techniques as there are art quilters. The important thing for you, as an artist, is to take ideas and methods from different sources and combine them, add to them, change them until you have developed your own unique style, your own voice.

The exercises in this book and on the accompanying DVD are meant to help you build the skills you will need to create your own artwork. You'll learn about composition, color, value and using thread painting for your detail work—and how to add your own vision and personality to create your own art.

HOW TO USE THIS BOOK

Creating art in any medium is a highly personal endeavor. No two people work in exactly the same way, nor is every artist drawn to the same subjects. Art quilting is no different than any other art form—you will bring to it your own vision, your own experiences and your own voice.

This book outlines the way I have decided to work as an art quilter. But keep in mind that, there are many different techniques, many different ways to solve the same problems, many ways to complete a project. I can only teach you what works for me.

Personally, I do not do any surface design or embellishment—no painting, stamping, dying, beading. This is a personal choice, but does not mean that I do not appreciate and admire quilts that include these techniques. And it is entirely possible that, in my own journey as an artist, I will begin to use some of these in my art. Art is not static; as artists we need to continue to improve and grow.

This book is intended to be a starting point, one of many sources of inspiration and instruction that you will use in your own journey as an artist. Learn from other books, as well. Take classes if you can. Don't be satisfied just completing the few quilts in this book. Expand on the ideas in this book and use them to develop your own style and voice.

Learn from this book and then make decisions about how you want to approach the creative process. You may decide that you have a more efficient or easier way to do something than I have described, and that is great. The idea behind this book is to start you on your path and give you some basic tools. These techniques and ideas are not hard and fast rules. What works for you is all that matters.

Most importantly, enjoy the process. I always tell my students that the process is key. When young children do a drawing or painting, they happily hand it over to anyone who admires it. Why? Because, for them, it is all about the process, the end result is unimportant. Don't stress about your results— enjoy the process, have fun and relax. If the process is satisfying to you, the end results will be, too.

NOTES FROM NANCY

As part of the **Create With Nancy** line, this book contains extra, helpful tips and a bonus DVD from sewing and craft expert Nancy Zieman. When you encounter a Note from Nancy, stop to read it! And be sure to watch the DVD to see the techniques in action!

Flamingos 15" × 14½

The supplies needed to create art quilts aren't entirely different from those needed for other types of quilting. Take a minute to look through this section for an overview of the materials you will need. Most of these items are easy to find, but if your local fabric store doesn't carry them, check out the resource list in the back of the book.

Sewing Machine

Art quilts, like any other sewing project, require a sewing machine in good working order. If your machine hasn't visited a technician in a while, take it in for cleaning and servicing.

There is no requirement for special features on a sewing machine in order to do art quilts, but a darning foot is necessary for thread painting, and a quilting foot is helpful in doing the final functional quilting.

A darning foot is designed to float over the surface of your fabric so you can move the fabric any way you wish. Look for one that has a large opening or is clear plastic, so you can see through them it working.

A quilting foot will allow the machine to move easily over the three layers of your final quilt and prevent puckering. For some sewing machines, only the brand designed for that machine will fit, but for the vast majority of machines, a relatively inexpensive generic can be used. When shopping for a generic foot, know the shank size of your machine. If you think of the sewing machine foot as a foot, then the shank is the leg attached to that foot. Shanks are high, low or slanted. If you aren't sure which one your machine needs, unscrew the shank and foot and bring them with you to the store.

Thread

For the basic construction of your art quilt, use white, gray or black thread for your bobbin and monofilament thread in both clear and smoke for your functional surface sewing. An assortment of colors for thread painting will be discussed later in the book. Good quality thread makes a big difference in the operation of your sewing machine, so don't skimp and buy unknown brands from the bargain bin. Polyester or polyblend threads in the bobbin will create less dust in your bobbin area than cotton thread.

Needles

The success of any sewing project often depends on using the right needle for the job. Since your art quilt will be predominately cotton, an 80/12 sharp needle is a good choice. Other sizes that may come in handy are 90/14 for thicker threads and a metallica needle for use with metallic threads. Remember to change the needle with each new project.

Fabric

Later we will discuss the kinds of fabrics you should begin to collect for your art quilts. Your favorite quilt shop is still the place to go, but you will be looking for fabrics that have an interesting surface design rather than bold beautiful prints. But don't despair; there are many fabrics in your current stash that will be great in your art quilts.

Batting

As with any other type of quilt, batting is a matter of personal choice. Some people prefer polyester batting, while others prefer cotton or poly/cotton blends. I do recommend that you use a thinner batting for your artwork (like traditional weight), and batting that is sold by the yard is more economical for the various finished sizes you will be creating.

Scissors

You'll need a good sharp pair of scissors that are only used for fabric and another pair that can be used for paper. If you use the same scissors for paper and fabric, they will not be sharp enough for a clean cut on fabric. A small pointed-end scissors for cutting tiny pieces of fabric is also very helpful.

Rotary Cutting Supplies

A medium sized rotary cutter with a ruler and cutting mat are useful for squaring off your final quilt.

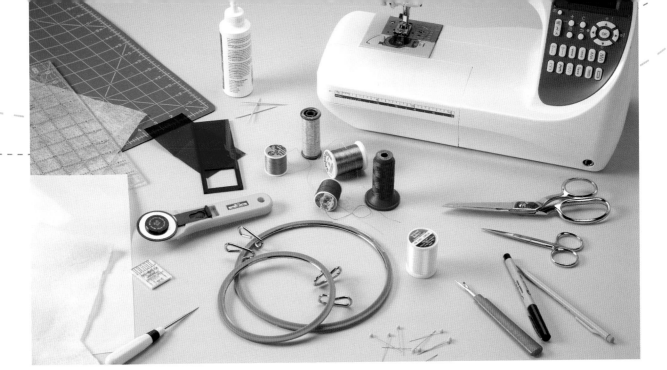

Pins

Like any other quilting project, you will need straight pins for both pinning the fabric alone and for pinning the fabric to your design wall. A magnetic pin cushion is a great way to keep all your pins in one place. In fact, I have three: one next to the sewing machine to receive the pins removed while sewing, one at the pressing table and one next to my design wall.

Foundation Material

I use Do-Sew, a material that is designed for making garment patterns, as the base of all my art quilts. It is lightweight, washable, can be ironed and cannot be torn. It's easy to trace the basic elements of my design onto Do-Sew and then glue or fuse all my collage pieces to it. I place this base over the batting, providing an easy way to transfer my work to the final step, and preventing "bearding" of batting onto dark fabric colors.

Red Plastic Viewer

A little rectangle of transparent red plastic or acetate may seem like an odd tool, but it's essential when trying to determine the relative values of different fabrics. You simply hold the viewer about six inches from your eyes, and look at the fabrics through it. You will not see the actual color anymore, just the value as they relate to each other. You can find red plastic viewers manufactured specifically for quilters—like the Ruby Beholder—or you can use a simple piece of red acetate.

Digital Camera

All of my quilts begin with a photo I've taken with my digital camera. I like being able to see all the details so that I don't have to figure out where the shadows would be, or the relative sizes and positioning of the elements. Many art quilters work from an idea in their heads or use other pictures for inspiration. The good news is that digital cameras are so reasonably priced these days that they don't require a big investment. I carry mine everywhere and keep the photos in computer files by type, such as "seascapes," for easy reference. I often combine photos as well, using Adobe Photoshop. Since I am only using the photo as a reference, a camera with lots of megapixels for clear enlargements is not essential.

Computer Equipment

Like the digital camera, this is a great help. I download the pictures, then manipulate them using photo-editing software. I use a scanner to scan images and print them on an ink jet printer. If you don't have a computer, you can still make beautiful art quilts.

Other Sewing Supplies

Your own sewing style will tell you if you need to have a seam ripper, stiletto, quilter's gloves, iron or appliqué press sheet. A few unconventional supplies include: freezer paper, tracing paper, fusible web, fabric glue and toothpicks, computer-printable foundation papers, computer-printable fabric, design wall (or large piece of foamcore) and binoculars or reducing glass.

BUILDING AN ART QUILT STASH

As quilters, we all have a passion for fabric, and most of us indulge that passion by creating a fabric stash. When collecting fabric for traditional quilts, the biggest question is always "how many yards do I buy?" and the answer is usually at least two or three yards, so that there will be enough to use in all the blocks and possibly the border of a quilt. The good news with art quilts is that you don't need to buy large amounts of the fabrics you collect, making it possible to build a bigger and better stash without buying multiple yards at a time. Most often, I purchase either a fat quarter, half yard or quarter yard, with the exception of fabrics that I think I will use a lot, use for backgrounds or use in making fairly large quilts. Even then, I rarely purchase more than a yard at a time.

Of course, it is possible to purchase the fabrics you need specifically for a particular art quilt. But the more fabrics you collect, the more options you will have when you just need that certain little piece. For the most part, you will begin to collect "textures" rather than prints. You will still be buying fabrics with prints, but you will be looking at them in a different way.

Resist the urge to purchase fabrics that already have an intention. Let's say you are doing an art quilt with rocks. There are many fabrics available with designs of rocks already printed on them. But chances are the scale of those rocks or the color will not be exactly right for your quilt, and even if it "fits," the quilt will be more interesting if you use an unexpected fabric for your rocks.

Also try not to purchase solid color fabrics. Sometimes, the only thing you can find that is the right color and value is a solid, but they are not as interesting in the finished art quilt as something that looks more complex. Instead of a solid color fabric for your quilt or your stash, look for one of the many batik, watercolor or "hand-dyed" look-a-likes which have multiple shades of that color, giving them more light and dark areas, and therefore making them more visually exciting—because they have a perceived "texture."

What you will begin to collect are either fabrics with small prints or fabrics that appear to have a surface texture. Look at the fabrics and think about whether they could be sky or water, grass or leaves, rocks or feathers. Most of the fabrics you buy can be more than one thing.

That is what makes your art quilts so much fun—that the same fabric can be used in so many ways. Collect your fabrics in color families. Grass or a landscape is not one color green, it is made up of many shades of green—so collect a lot of different green fabrics with different shades and textures. Seascapes, water and sky, are also made up of various shades of blue. The more fabrics you have to choose from, the easier the selection process will be while you are making your art quilts. If you look though the quilts in this book, you will begin to recognize many fabrics from my stash, used in different ways in the different quilts.

Once you bring your fabrics home, develop a system to sort them that works for you. I keep all similar tones in clear plastic storage bins—for example I have a bin for light blues, one for medium blues, one for dark blues and then other bins for blue/greens (like turquoise) also sorted into bins of light, medium and dark. That way, when I need to find the right fabric, I am not pulling out everything I own. If I find that a certain fabric "crosses over" into another bin, I often put some of it in each

TREASURES FROM MY STASH
The textures and patterns in my stash are extremely versatile. Think "outside the box" and use them in unexpected places.

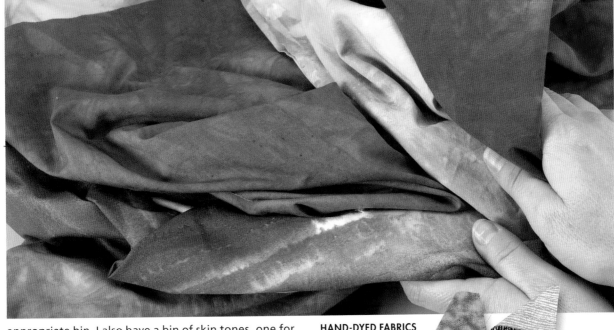

appropriate bin. I also have a bin of skin tones, one for tree bark and one for black and white fabrics. You'll need to sort out what you have in a way that makes sense for how you plan to use it.

Another component of a great stash is hand-dyed fabrics. There are many commercially available fabrics now that have the look of hand dyes, and I use those a lot. But true hand-dyed fabrics are like beautiful art themselves. I don't dye fabric myself, but every year I splurge and purchase one or two yards that I use primarily for very special backgrounds in my quilts. There is a richness to these fabrics that can't be found elsewhere.

If you're like me, you have lots of little calico prints that have been in your stash for a very long time. These fabrics aren't something I would use now in a more traditional quilt, but they're great in art quilts. And don't forget to turn your fabrics over; there are lots of wonderful surprises on the back!

The downside of working with art quilts rather than traditional ones, is that every little piece of fabric counts, and can be used somewhere. That means I never want to throw even the smallest pieces away. I have one bin that sits next to my design wall that I call "precious pieces" and it contains little scraps of all my favorite fabrics (including the small pieces left over when I cut into my hand-dyes). These small pieces are great in water, tree bark, hair, lots of places. I try to draw the line at saving anything smaller than 1" square, but have to admit that for favorite fabrics, even pieces smaller than that are often in my precious pieces stash!

HAND-DYED FABRICS

BEAUTIFUL, FRONT TO BACK

STORING YOUR FABRICS

Store your fabrics in a convenient location. I store mine under the cutting table in my studio and sort them logically by color.

15

A DESIGN WALL

Using a design wall makes a big difference, both in your ability to evaluate your art quilt as you work and in the size of your finished pieces. This wall allows me to hang not only the quilt I am working on, but other pictures for reference, pieces of fabric and other small items that might get lost. It also serves as the perfect background for photographing your finished art quilts.

Until I moved into a large enough room to put up a design wall, my art quilts were limited to the size of my table top. There is nothing wrong with doing art quilts this size, but for flexibility, if you are lucky enough to have a dedicated sewing space, a design wall is a great help.

If you don't have a dedicated sewing area, you still have a couple of options. One is to put up a design wall in the room you use for your sewing, and when you aren't using it as a design wall, you can pin up one of your finished quilts as wall decor!

Also consider using a single sheet of foamcore as a portable design wall. Choose a size that will fit comfortably on the table you plan to use for your design work. Unlike the design wall, where you would be working vertically, your work will be done onto the foamcore while it rests flat on the table. You can pin directly into it, just like the wall, and when you need to step back and evaluate your work, simply prop it up and step back to see your art quilt develop.

I have also put a picture hook next to my design wall to hold my binoculars, so they are always right there when I need them to step back and evaluate.

MY STUDIO'S DESIGN WALL
My design wall is my work surface when I'm putting together my quilts. I can pin up swatches, sketches and photos that I want to have nearby for reference.

ON A SMALLER SCALE
If you're lacking space, a single foamcore board will work well. Just prop it up on a chair and step back evaluate as your work progresses.

Stop and Evaluate

To evaluate your progress, use a pair of binoculars backwards to view your quilt, so that you are making the view smaller. This is like stepping far back; you'll see immediately what isn't working. Reviewing digital photos on the computer screen also works.

Easy Design Wall

There are lots of ways to build a design wall and a variety of materials you can use. The most cost-effective and simple way to do it is to use white foamcore and picture-hanging nails. Large sheets of foamcore are not very expensive and can hold up to pinning for a long time. Because they are lightweight, they are easily held in place with picture hanging nails, which will not damage your walls. I hung my own design wall in half an hour—by myself.

Over time, you'll find that the foamcore in the center section of your wall gets "chewed up" by the pins before the rest. You can gently remove these sheets from the wall and flip them over to use the other side. When a piece of foamcore is too bad to use anymore, simply replace it with a new one the same size by removing it and putting a new one right in its place.

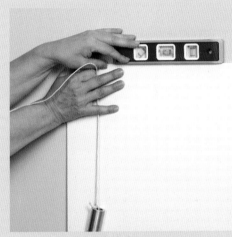

1 Measure the wall to decide how many sheets of foamcore (and in what sizes) you will need.

Starting at the bottom of your foamcore wall, mark where the sheets will go. Use a level and a plumb line (mine is simply a long piece of string with a double knot at the top and a piece of metal at the bottom) to ensure you hang them straight. Mark the placement with a pencil.

2 Starting at the bottom of your foamcore wall, hang the foamcore sheets one at a time. (Keep checking the placement with the level and plumb line.) You will need to put one picture-hanging nail in each corner of every sheet, and also in the center of the long sides so that everything is held tightly in place.

The cardboard covering on the foamcore can eventually break around the nail, allowing it to slide off. To prevent this, put a small piece of selvage cut from cotton fabric—about 1" square—between the foamcore and each nail. Continue until all your foamcore sheets are in place.

Keeping Things in Line

The plumb line can serve as a great vertical reference when your design wall is complete. I often pin the knot onto the design wall above the quilt, and the metal piece at the bottom insures that the string hangs straight, giving me the perfect vertical reference line.

LIGHTLY TOASTED   28" x 22"

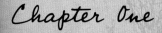

Chapter One

THE ELEMENTS OF GOOD DESIGN

It does not matter how beautiful your fabric selection is or the skill you bring to your technique, if your composition is not interesting, your art quilt will not be as exciting as it could be.

To find inspiration for good design, begin by turning to your collection of snapshots and photographs. A snapshot is what its name implies: a quick snap of the camera to capture a moment in time. Often snapshots are of friends and family, our pets or things we want to remember in our travels. A photograph, on the other hand, can be an artwork by itself, taking into consideration overall composition, lighting, mood and expression. Your starting photo may be a snapshot, but you want to evaluate all the elements in the picture and decide what stays and what goes. You want the viewer to focus in on a certain element, and anything distracting needs to be removed.

The good news is that even a snapshot can serve as the guide for a great art quilt. You don't need an expensive camera; in fact, your photo doesn't even need to be in focus to make a great art quilt! Because your photo is just a guide, you can crop for greater impact, change things you don't like, move elements around and leave out distractions. You can even make a beautiful art quilt in full color from a black and white photo. All you really need are the essential elements of good design to set a mood and tell a story.

CHOOSING THE **SUBJECT** AND TELLING A STORY

The first step in creating an art quilt is choosing your subject. It's often said of writing that you should "write what you know." This is true of artwork, too. It's best to work with subjects that have a connection, or an emotional appeal, to you personally. This brings part of you into the artwork and makes it your personal expression.

If you aren't moved by flowers, don't do them. If faces are what fascinate you, work on faces. Make art quilts of places you have been or to express your feelings. Be true to what your inner voice tells you. I just know when a certain image has to be my next art quilt. Trust your instincts.

After you have chosen a subject for your art quilt, think about the feeling you wish to convey about that subject. Any artwork that tells the viewer a story is more compelling and invites them to become more involved in looking at the artwork.

Ask yourself: What is the story behind this subject? What is the mood? Is there another element that would help to tell the story that should be included in the overall design? The answers to these questions will determine many aspects of your art quilt, like the format, color and selection of fabric. There is a reason you were drawn to this subject; think about what that reason is and how to communicate that to your viewer using your artwork as your voice.

AN OUTSTRETCHED HAND   30" x 21½"

CAPTURING THE STORY OF A LIFE
Many years ago, I studied for my MA degree in Florence, Italy. This woman regularly begged for money on the street where I lived. In my arrogant youth, I took a photo of her before I returned home, but I don't remember ever giving her money. I have always felt guilty about that, and only recently decided to honor her by making the photo into an art quilt. I tried to capture her pain—an elderly woman who must once have had hopes and dreams, but who was forced to live a life she hadn't chosen.

DIVIDING THE **COMPOSITION**

Rather than splitting your composition in the center, or centering your focal point, it is much more interesting to employ the ⅓ : ⅔ approach to composition.

Let's say you are creating a landscape. If you place the horizon line right in the middle of your design, the result will be dull and uninteresting. If you move that horizon line up or down, you can change the focus. If you shift the line up, so that you have ⅓ sky and ⅔ land, the land becomes the subject of the piece. If the sky occupies ⅔ of the composition and the land only ⅓, then the sky becomes the more important element.

This asymmetrical balance creates more interest and invites the viewer to look around the artwork. The same is true when planning your design from side to side. An off-centered, asymmetrical composition is more intriguing than planting your focal point smack in the center of your artwork with nowhere else for the eye to travel.

It's also important to consider the spaces between your design elements, or the negative space. These areas are called negative space because they do not represent any particular design elements. But they are just as important as the design elements to the overall composition. It is often the negative space that helps form your ⅓ to ⅔ composition.

HORIZON LINE DOWN THE MIDDLE
Here, the horizon line runs through the center, splitting the scene in half. It's an uninspiring, static composition.

HORIZON LINE SHIFTED UP
The horizon line shifts up, making the land, creek and bridge the focus. The ⅓ to ⅔ ratio is here, making the composition more dynamic.

HORIZON LINE SHIFTED DOWN
The horizon line shifts down, but keeps the dynamic ⅓ to ⅔ split. Here, the trees and their bright leaves are the focus.

CHOOSING THE RIGHT FORMAT: HORIZONTAL VERSUS VERTICAL

For the most part, compositions that are horizontal in orientation—that is wider than tall, like a horizon line—tend to evoke a feeling of calm and restfulness. Vertical compositions—meaning that they are taller than they are wide—give more of a feeling of action and emphasize vertical lines, giving the artwork a sense of height. Your choice of vertical or horizontal format can often change the mood of your art quilt. There is immediacy to vertical compositions, whereas horizontal compositions seem to depict time standing still.

NOTES FROM NANCY

It may be tempting to use a professional photograph or a famous art piece as the pattern for your art quilt. Keep in mind the copyright rules. Unless a photo or art piece is public domain, it is not yours for the choosing. Appreciate the scenes around you and the convenience of a digital camera to capture your original pattern!

PINE BROOK   21" × 27"

VERTICAL FORMAT

PINE BROOK (above) depicts a scene near my house, a lovely brook running through a grove of trees. By orienting this image in a vertical format, the trees seem taller, and the brook becomes the focal point that leads the eye into the composition. If it had been a horizontal format, the brook disappearing into the horizon would not have been so prominent; the trees would not appear so tall.

HORIZONTAL FORMAT

A horizontal format is almost necessary in TOURIST SEASON (left) because I had to fit everyone in one image, but it also gives a sense of repose—these people are standing and listening, not moving in space. By making this horizontal, I was also able to show a minimal amount of background, making the people the important part of the artwork.

TOURIST SEASON   45½" × 34"

USING **LINES**: HORIZONTAL, VERTICAL, DIAGONAL OR CURVED

Horizontal and vertical lines within your artwork have the same effect as they do in format. Using horizontal lines in your design will make it appear calm and reposed; they are often used in landscapes and seascapes for just that reason, the restful beauty of nature. Vertical lines cause the eye to move up and down the artwork, creating a sense of energy.

Diagonal lines suggest motion and movement, like something darting across the surface. By contrast, gently curving lines bring the eye slowly into the picture, evoking a feeling of grace and beauty.

COLONNADE   12" × 22"

HEADED HOME   35½" × 24½"

DIAGONAL LINES

HEADED HOME shows a central figure walking towards a commuter train in a station. The strong diagonal lines of the train and the ceiling make the otherwise static figure appear to be moving down the platform. Diagonal lines pull the eye into the composition, creating lots of movement.

VERTICAL AND CURVED LINES

In COLONNADE, the vertical lines draw the eye up, creating a sense of energy. By using an eye level that is low in the columns, we are looking up at them, increasing the sense of height. The curved line of the arches caps the composition with a calm elegance.

TAKING BETTER SNAPSHOTS

When shooting snapshots, most people often instinctively stand straight on and shoot the picture that way. But this is not always the most interesting angle. Sometimes, just moving slightly to one side makes a much more intriguing picture. Shooting from lower or higher than eye level or moving just a few feet to one side in order to change perspective can produce a more unique and unusual angle and, therefore, a more artistic viewpoint. Very often an unexpected view is all that is needed to make something mundane into something creative and artistic.

When taking pictures to be used in art quilts, take several if you can. Move in close so there is a strong focal point without much distraction. Move around to get different viewpoints so that you can decide later on which one (or which elements from each) works best.

STANDARD SNAPSHOT (ABOVE)
This photo is a standard snapshot. The tree is the focus of the shot, but there's so much going on around it, it gets lost. There's nothing that draws the eye, nothing that makes an artistic statement.

BETTER (RIGHT)
By shifting your perspective slightly, the two trunks of the tree (previously in a very wide "V") move into a more appealing relationship to each other. We no longer see that gaping space between them; they appear to be complementing each other. Closing in on the subject also gives more of a sense of the tree, with less of the distracting background.

BEST (LEFT)
Moving even closer to the tree reveals the beautiful texture of the bark, the thin branches that radiate out of the trunk and just a hint of the trees in the background. We don't need to see the entire tree to know what it is. Notice that it is slightly to one side of the composition rather than in the center. Compare this "art" shot to the "snapshot" we started with. It was simply a matter of moving closer and slightly shifting the angle.

CROPPING CLOSE FOR IMPACT

Frequently, the biggest difference between a snapshot and a great photo is how much space the subject occupies. The most common mistake people make in taking snapshots is that the subject of the photo is centered and too small, with lots of unnecessary and distracting "space" around it. Moving in close when taking your photo, or cropping your snapshot to eliminate all of this unnecessary or empty space is one of the most important things you can do to create an art quilt with impact and drama.

Cropping can also change the overall composition so that the position of the central element in relation to the rest of the environment is more appealing. Even if the original photo centered the focal point, cropping can change the vision to a ⅓ : ⅔ viewpoint.

It is easy to crop a photo using a computer program. If you are not working on the computer, print your photo and cut it so that you eliminate the parts you don't want.

THE FOCAL POINT

I took this shot of my son, Jordan, playing his guitar in my very cluttered studio. Clearly, the background does nothing for the photo; it's distracting and irrelevant (though I like the way the light highlighted one side of his face). By cropping out the background, I was able to make this a quilt of him alone. Cropping off the top of his head, his right arm and the guitar neck focuses the attention on his face looking down at the guitar strings.

Watch the Joints

When cropping people or animals in your artwork, always crop just above or just below a joint—like a knee or elbow. Cropping *at* the joint will make the limb look amputated.

JORDAN   29" × 28"

25

PERSPECTIVE

Perspective, an element of design that makes objects in your composition seem to disappear into the distance, can also bring visual interest to your artwork. A building depicted straight on will have horizontal and vertical lines at its edges. If you move slightly to one side, those horizontal lines become diagonal lines, as you see the building in perspective. Remember that diagonal lines are more dynamic and horizontal lines are more static. Since perspective lines always converge at the horizon line, they are also an effective way to draw the eye into the composition.

LIFE WAS SIMPLER WHEN ALL I NEEDED WAS TEDDY   19" x 27"

STAIRS   14" x 21½"

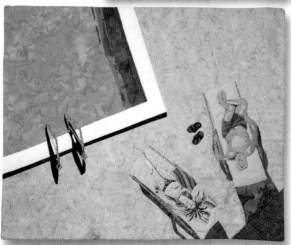

LIGHTLY TOASTED   28" x 22"

VIEWING THE SUBJECT STRAIGHT ON

LIFE WAS SIMPLER WHEN ALL I NEEDED WAS TEDDY has a perspective that is straight-on—there are no diagonal lines that indicate dimension or depth. This was a conscious decision. I wanted to portray the time in a person's life when there are no worries, when life is about simple things. The straight forward perspective supports this; the extreme height of the door in relation to the boy (my older son, Jared, when he was young) emphasizes how small he is.

VIEWING THE SUBJECT FROM BELOW

In STAIRS, the boy (my younger son, Jordan, as a child) is seated on a flight of stairs. Stairs are a wonderful way to show depth and dimension. The angle of the stairs leads the eye to the door behind him. This more complex composition is fitting for a quilt that expresses more complex emotions. What is he thinking? Is he contemplative, upset? This is for the viewers to decide (although I know exactly what was going on at the time!).

VIEWING THE SUBJECT FROM ABOVE

LIGHTLY TOASTED is a relatively mundane subject—two people on lounge chairs by a pool—but the viewing angle is unexpected, which makes the composition more interesting. Angling the corner of the pool, instead of placing it along the horizontal and vertical lines of the piece, also adds an element of surprise. My favorite detail in this quilt are the sandals, seen so clearly from above, which would be barely visible at eye level.

LEADING THE EYE IN

Another important trick used by artists and photographers is leading the eye in to the composition. Usually starting at the bottom of the composition—a road, a path, a fence, even a color—can bring the viewer into the design and usually ends at either the focal point or horizon line. Leading the eye in can create a sense of depth and distance, as the eye travels in and around the composition.

A strong visual element at the bottom front or one or both sides can do the same thing, a technique called "framing." Often in landscapes, there is a tree or branch in the foreground that acts as a frame for the landscape in the distance. Other common visual elements used for framing include doors, windows or gates. Framing can add instant dimension to your composition by creating the illusion of distance.

SUSPICION   13¼" × 20"

DIAGONAL LINES

The figure in the corner is the first thing the viewer sees. But the diagonal line of the street, and the dark figure on the other side by the shop, serve to draw the viewer's attention into the composition. The diagonal line of the roofline also serves to pull the eye towards the arch and the men standing underneath it. A thin line of sunlight in front of the men also pulls the eye toward the back.

FRAMING THE SUBJECT

This quilt depicts a boy at the age when he feels the need to challenge himself rather than rely on his parents. That is why the foreground is dark and the background is light—he is leaving the light and entering the unknown. The light, the arch shape and the lighter area at his feet pull the eye towards the central figure. Viewers have the sense that they are moving through a dark tunnel towards the boy, who is framed by the arch.

CHALLENGE   20" × 29"

WORKING WITH ODD NUMBERS

Just as breaking your composition into 1/3 : 2/3 is more compelling than a composition that is split 50/50, the same is true for the number of elements in your artwork. Odd numbers of items are more interesting than even numbers. Three apples will be a more interesting composition than two. Five will be more interesting than four. Anything that breaks up your space in an asymmetrical manner will create more drama and excitement.

This does not necessarily mean that you must have three of the same thing or that your objects need to be the same size. Groupings of odd numbers will create the same sort of asymmetry as the 1/3 : 2/3 division of space, inviting the eye to move around the artwork.

DIFFERENT HEIGHTS

Now that you have decided to use three (or more) design elements in your artwork, make them even more interesting by varying their height. This is a variation of leading the eye in—as the eye travels up and down to the tops of these vases, the viewer takes in more of the artwork.

NOTES FROM NANCY

If you sew traditional quilts, these same composition rules apply to patchwork designs! If you think about it, the 1/3 : 2/3 rule is incorporated into many traditional quilt blocks—9-Patch, Triple Rail Fence, Irish Chain and more! Regardless of the quilt topic, Leni's suggestions apply.

PLACING THE **VISUAL WEIGHT**

In the Western world, we read from left to right. For this reason, our brains are trained to see from left to right when looking at art. Because of this, it is most natural for us to view art that requires the eye to travel from the left of the composition to the right, often with the heaviest element on the right side.

Most importantly, the placement of the visual weight becomes a vehicle for splitting your composition into ⅓ : ⅔ and drawing the eye into or around the artwork.

In an artwork where the visual weight sits firmly in the center of the composition, there is no need for the eye to travel around, so the artwork will not be as compelling.

THE BALLOON MAN TAKES A BREAK   21¼" × 22½"

VISUAL WEIGHT ON THE LEFT

THE BALLOON MAN TAKES A BREAK appears to be the opposite of the composition rule, with the figure on the left. But in this case, as there is something else to look at, the eye is drawn into the composition and we are invited to look over his shoulder to see what he is seeing. The man acts like a frame, not unlike a tree branch leading the eye into a distant landscape. The background becomes an important part of the story in this quilt; if it were not (as in THE VOID) the eye would be led into nothing.

VISUAL WEIGHT TO THE RIGHT

In THE VOID, the seated figure is at the right side of the composition. The shadow draws the eye from the left edge of the quilt to the figure, requiring a visual journey across the surface of the artwork. If the figure had been placed on the left with the shadow on the right, the eye would be led away to nothing, eventually falling off the edge of the quilt on the other side.

THE VOID   24½" × 19½"

29

DEPICTING LIGHT AND SHADOW

One of the advantages of working from a photograph when making your art quilt is that you don't have to figure out where the light source and shadows should be. Light and shadow help define contour and shape. They are also the two extremes of value and a great way to bring those value variations into your art quilt.

Remember that if you combine photos you must keep the light source and shadows consistent. If the light comes from the right, the shadows appear on the left and vice versa. If the light shines down from the top, the shadows are on the bottom, and vice versa. If the light is straight on (like high noon) there will be almost no shadow at all. Clouds also cause shadows to fall on landscapes, adding a sense of dimension to landscapes.

LIGHT FROM OVERHEAD
When the light source is directly overhead, like high noon, the shadows fall below the objects. This can be particularly unflattering for people, as strong shadows appear below the nose, chin and even under the eyes.

LIGHT FROM THE LEFT
Side lighting is more flattering to faces and creates more interesting shadows for other objects. The light and dark areas of the background are more artistic than a flatly lit background.

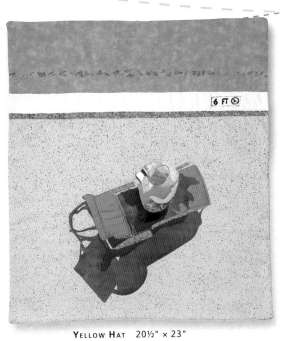

Yellow Hat 20½" × 23"

STRONG SHADOW

In Yellow Hat, the strong shadow helps tell the story—the time of day, the strong sunlight suggesting summer or a warm climate. Remember that value is often more important than color, so the purple shadow does not seem unnatural.

DESIGNING WITH SHADOW

Conflicted Provenance also has a shadow that becomes an important design element. We see the man only in shadow; to his right the shadow helps define the shape of the stairs, and both lead the eye up to the arches.

CREATING RELATIONSHIPS

In Tourist Season, shadows also form an integral part of the composition, linking the people and suggesting strong early morning or late day sunlight. The shadows also help lead the eye from one side to the other.

Conflicted Provenance 14" × 20"

Tourist Season 45½" × 34"

31

UNDERSTANDING COLOR

There are three major characteristics of color: Hue, value and saturation.

Hue

Hue is simply the name of the color, regardless of whether it is light or dark. Red, green, orange, turquoise—any color name is actually its hue.

Value

Value refers to the lightness or darkness of a color. For instance, pink is a light value of red, and navy is a dark value of blue. Values are the light/medium/darks that create contrast in quilts and can be even more important for a successful art quilt than hue alone. Value is relative; a fabric that is a medium value in one quilt may be a dark in a different quilt, or even a light in another.

Saturation

Saturation (or intensity) is the degree of purity or clarity of the color. For example, bright red is highly saturated, while dusty rose is less saturated, even though they may be the same value. Think of saturation like dye—the more dye you put onto the fabric, the more intense and clear the color.

Temperature

Color temperature can be determined by both hue and saturation. The way hue affects temperature is obvious: Red, orange, yellow and the colors in between them on a color wheel are warm colors and will make your quilt look warm or energized, like the colors of fire. Blues, greens and purples are the opposite side of the color wheel and are cool, calm and restful. Combining temperatures can make your quilt vibrate.

Monochromatic colors

Using a single hue in a variety of values and saturations is a monochromatic color scheme. These combinations are soothing and restful (especially in cool colors like blue and green) but may be boring in artwork because there is nothing to add any particular visual excitement.

Analogous Colors

Using colors that are next to each other on the color wheel will also result in a mood that is serene, but with more subtle harmony than a monochromatic combination, as the colors blend together. A few example of analogous combinations are: blue and green; blue and green with a hint of purple; and red, orange and yellow.

Complementary Colors

Red and green, blue and orange, purple and yellow are all "complementary colors" which means they are opposite each other on the color wheel and will "pop" when used together.

Using complementary colors in your quilt will create a sort of visual vibration. A predominantly red quilt with just touch of green will come alive, as will a blue quilt with even a tiny bit of orange. In part, this results from mixing warm and cool colors, but is most effective when the colors are directly opposite each other on the color wheel.

You need only add a hint of the complementary color for effect, and often the complement works best if used in a different value (think about pink roses with green leaves).

Using Color to Create Distance

The proper use of color can also help you depict distance. Consider a landscape with mountains in the distance. The farther away the mountains, the lighter and greyer they appear. So a mountain done in a dark fabric will appear closer, and one done in a lighter, grayer tone will look farther away. This is true of anything that you want to recede into the distance—the farther back it goes, the lighter, grayer and cooler the color of fabric you should use to depict it.

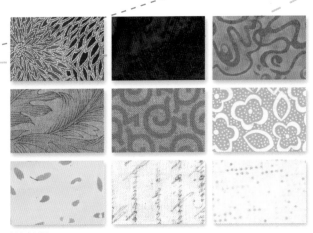

HUE
These swatches vary in saturation and value, but they all have the same hue: they are blue.

VALUE
In this group, the top row shows the darkest values, and the bottom shows the lightest values.

SATURATION
The range of colors above vary, but are all very saturated colors. The blue-gray square above is less saturated.

ZINGERS
A zinger is a fabric that, although it is predominantly the right color and value, has a lot of other colors or patterns in it. Too many zingers will be visually confusing, but including one or two in places that will not dominate the other fabrics can add a little unexpected surprise to the mix.

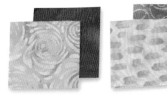

COMPLEMENTARY COLORS
These coupled swatches are complementary colors. Complementary colors are color opposites: Orange and blue; green and red; purple and yellow. Put them near each other, and they create a strong reaction.

Don't forget to look at the backs of your fabrics as well. Sometimes the back is just the value or color you are looking for!

TOURIST SEASON   45½" × 34"

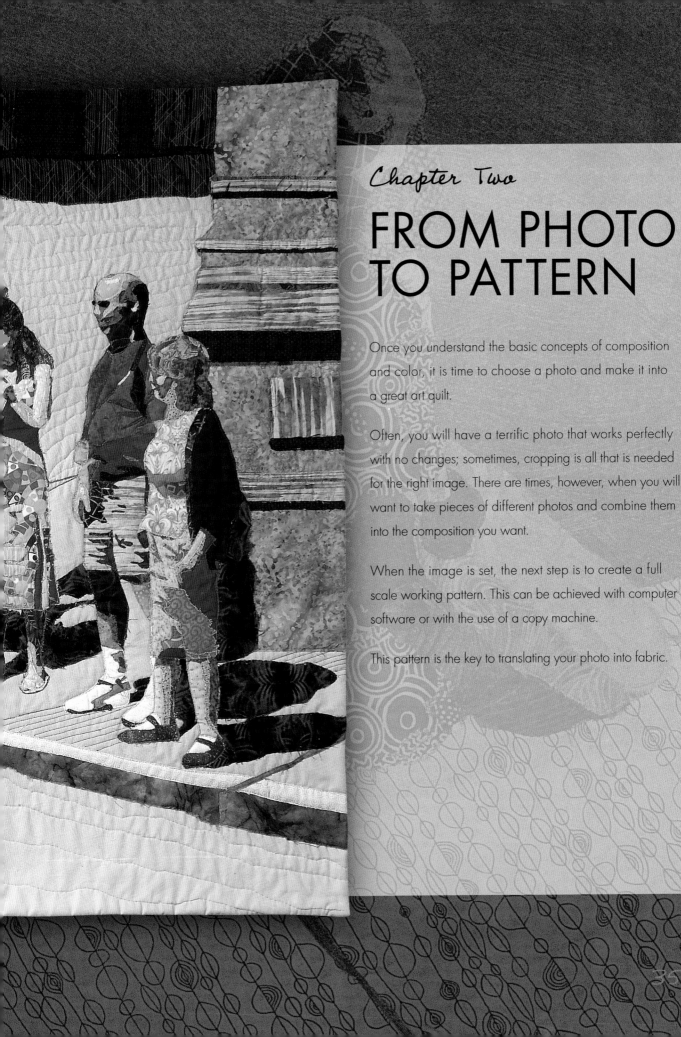

Chapter Two

FROM PHOTO TO PATTERN

Once you understand the basic concepts of composition and color, it is time to choose a photo and make it into a great art quilt.

Often, you will have a terrific photo that works perfectly with no changes; sometimes, cropping is all that is needed for the right image. There are times, however, when you will want to take pieces of different photos and combine them into the composition you want.

When the image is set, the next step is to create a full scale working pattern. This can be achieved with computer software or with the use of a copy machine.

This pattern is the key to translating your photo into fabric.

COMBINING PHOTOS FOR
BETTER COMPOSITION

As I wander around with my camera, snapping images that I think will make great art quilts, I often find that what I get is not exactly what I want for my art quilt. Often, the composition is not quite right, and in those cases, I look for other photos that may have objects or people I can use. Since I keep all of my photos in files on my computer, organized by type—landscapes, people, buildings, animals, etc.—I can always locate what I need.

Because you're creating your own artistic vision, it is not necessary to remain true to the original photograph. Combining elements from different photos is the way you bring your own creative idea to life.

TELLING A STRONGER STORY

I love the way this woman was draped over the rock with the water in the background. Because the man in the photo is kneeling, the composition is not as interesting as it could be. I wanted him standing looking out at the water, so that the eye is drawn in. I was able to take one of the figures from the second photo and place him on the rock. I like this composition much better.

ON THE ROCKS   28" × 37½"

36

STAIRS 14" × 21½"

FILLING IN THE SETTING

I loved the intensity of my son in this photo, but was bothered by the empty looking space at the top of the stairs. By adding another photo of a beautiful door, the eye is drawn to something interesting. Moving the boy slightly over to one side creates a more pleasing ⅓ : ⅔ spacing.

When I worked with Leni to plan and tape the DVD, I became the student. The lesson in combining of photos was an **a-ha** moment for me! I've combined quilt patterns, yet it didn't occur to me to combine photos. The value of this exercise is immediately clear just seeing two photos and the final quilt.

Combining Photos

Here is a series of five snapshots taken by my son at a zoo. No one shot is perfect for an art quilt. Let's examine them each of them to determine which elements are worth saving, and how to combine them into one great art quilt.

There's no right or wrong choice; this is where your artistic vision, and what you want to say about the flamingos is important.

Photoediting

Photos are easily combined using photoediting software like Adobe Photoshop or Adobe Photoshop Elements. If you don't have access to these programs, simply print the photos you want and cut and paste to get the result you want. Think about making some enlarged copies so the elements are the right scale.

PHOTO 1

I like the way the tree at the front left frames the composition, and I like the graceful S-curve of the water into the back. The flamingo on the right is perfect; we see him clearly, and the curve of his neck as he drinks water is lovely. The flamingo next to him is another matter; we only see the back of him and not even enough to be certain what we are looking at. He has to go. This is the only photo in the group where the water has a beautiful blue tone; the others are all very brown and unappealing. For that reason, I'll refer to this photo as a guide for color regardless of composition.

PHOTO 2

This is a great shot of a flamingo. We can feel him moving forward. The height of his legs and neck and the movement of the water all work well. There's too much empty space around him, however, which does nothing for the composition, and a vertical rather than horizontal format would accentuate his long legs and long neck.

PHOTO 3

Although there are many individual flamingos that would work well in an art quilt, and the diagonal line of the sand and water's edge is nice, there's just too much going on in here. The eye is not drawn in; there are so many directions to go that the overall effect is chaos. I do like the way the flamingos in the front of the picture frame the composition.

PHOTO 4

There is a nice curve of the water's edge leading the eye into the horizon line, but beyond that there isn't much about this shot that works well. The multitude of birds all clumped together makes an interesting color compliment to the green behind them, but because so few have their necks up, we lose a sense that they are flamingos.

PHOTO 5

There's too much going on for the eye to take in at once, but the gentle curve of the sand leading the eye to the bridge at the back is nice. The greenery at the front bottom also acts as a frame to the picture. There are several flamingos in good positions if isolated.

FINAL VERSION

This final version combines all the elements I liked in the others, particularly the curved neck of the drinking flamingo (and the ripples in the water where his beak touches the surface). The juxtaposition of the two birds is more interesting than either alone The foreground helps frame the composition. Some elements, like the ducks, will be removed because they don't add anything to the composition.

Cropping

As discussed earlier, cropping can make the difference between a picture and an artwork. This is not to say that an image isn't perfect just the way it is, but there are lots of ways to crop it, each creating a very different result.

EMPHASIZING THE STORY

I loved this photo of a clown enjoying a private moment. I only used the upper part of his body, as that made a stronger statement and led nicely into the background he is observing without all the "empty" space of the road around his legs. In making him bright and the background just gray and white and sketchy, emphasized his detachment from the action around him. The addition of the cigarette (not in the original photo) seemed to support the sense that this is really just a man taking a break from his job.

THE BALLOON MAN TAKES A BREAK   21¼" × 22½"

THE ENDLESS DANCE OF THE PONYTAIL   29¼" × 30"

THE DRAMATIC FOCUS

While having lunch in a local café, I was fascinated by this group of teenagers at the next table. The girl with her back to me was constantly taking her hair in and out of a rubber band. The endless upward movement of her arms reminded me of a flamenco dancer. By cropping out everything around her, her dance became the central focus of the art quilt—far more interesting than a crowd of people.

ELIMINATING THE UN-ESSENTIAL

The photo is a nice overview shot (and I like that tree on the right) but cropping in closer made the man in shadow the focal point, framed by the beautiful arches and the mosque behind them. The long shadow on the stairs is now a star of the composition, whereas it was somewhat lost in the full photo.

CONFLICTED PROVENANCE   14" x 20"

PATIENCE   29" x 40"

FOCUSING THE ATTENTION

I love to take random photos of people in unremarkable moments in their lives. This photo of people sitting on the steps of the New York Public Library will ultimately serve as the base for several art quilts. Cropping in around the one woman on the steps next to the lion focuses attention on her, as opposed to placing all the people in the composition, which means none of them are the focal point. I am careful to change the appearance of strangers so as not to invade anyone's privacy.

SIZE MATTERS

The size of your finished artwork will have a definite impact. A very large piece demands attention; it has power and strength just because of its presence. But that does not mean that a small piece, one that requires the viewer to move in close in order to examine it, cannot have power and presence.

The reality is that the size of the pieces you produce is dependant in large part by the space in which you work. Producing pieces that are six feet square requires a design wall that size and could not be accomplished on the top of your kitchen table. For many years, before I had a dedicated studio space with a design wall, my art quilts were never larger than a single sheet of foam core, which I used as my portable design wall.

Trying to work too small can present problems. If you decide to begin with a quilt of an image printed onto a single sheet of paper (about 8" × 10"), you will be quickly frustrated by the tiny pieces you need to cut and place in your work. For this reason, I recommend that a good starting size is equivalent to four sheets of paper. That means that the photo is printed so that each quarter of the image is on a single sheet and they are combined to make a piece that is roughly 16" × 20". This is a manageable size and looks significant when finished.

If you do choose to begin with an art quilt much smaller than that, choose an image that will not have an abundance of tiny pieces to cut and place. A simple design with fewer pieces will be easier to accomplish (especially in the beginning) than one that is highly complex. The scale of your image should be appropriate for the size of your art quilt.

WORKING IN THE RIGHT SIZE

Often, the size of your finished art quilt is a function of the space you have to work in, and sometimes it is a decision based on other factors. The quilt of the woman's face is effective in a small size because it is a close-up. The quilt beneath it, TOURIST SEASON, needed to be large enough for me to be able to show detail in each of the many people pictured.

AUTUMN   16" × 20"

NOTES FROM **NANCY**

To begin your **Photo-Inspired Art Quilts** venture, consider using one of Leni's patterns that are included on pages 103 to 123. The size of these patterns is ideal for a first project, plus there are many topics to choose, from landscape to still life.

WORKING SMALL

In this small art quilt, the details are more impressionistic than realistic, making it easy to use little snippets of fabric. Had I made this quilt large, those pieces of fabric would have looked like randomly cut pieces and would not have blended as nicely into each other.

WORKING LARGE

For JORDAN, I wanted a dramatic impression, so I made the quilt large. This also allowed me to faithfully depict all the details of the guitar (something that was very important to my son). Although the face and hand would have made an effective art quilt in a smaller size, the fact that they are life size has a presence that a smaller quilt would have lacked.

JORDAN   29" × 28"

43

USING PHOTOEDITING FILTERS TO CREATE A **PATTERN**

A computer isn't necessary to make an art-quilt pattern (many quilters draw patterns by hand), but I've found that the filters in photoediting software help simplify images into manageable parts. The cutout filter, for example, reduces the number of colors visible so that you have more defined areas to cut from fabric. The downside is that in reducing the number of colors, the program often combines pieces you didn't want combined, or shifts colors. I work with Adobe Photoshop or Adobe Photoshop Elements, but most photoediting programs have similar features. Learning to play with the program so that you can get the pattern you want takes some practice.

The Cutout Filter

The cutout filter in Photoshop or Photoshop Elements is a very good choice for creating an easy-to-use pattern from your photo (it's what I used to create the patterns at the back of the book). Basically, the filter reduces the hundreds of colors present in the photo to just a few, making a clear distinction for cutting shapes from fabric. The further you reduce the number of colors, the more simplistic the image becomes, so reducing too far will eliminate all detail. For that reason, I use the "levels" setting in the filter at the highest number (8) so that I get the most detail. Often, I find that I have to segregate sections of the photo to apply the filter a bit at a time in order to maintain detail.

Other Filter Options

Although the cutout filter is the one that most often gives me a good pattern, there are cases when other filters work better. You may prefer another filter to the cutout filter, or you may like to use a combination of filters for different photos. The filters I find most helpful in Adobe Photoshop are: Artistic—poster edges; Brushstrokes—ink outlines; and Brushstrokes—accented edges.

After you've selected your filters, experiment with cropping and adjusting both the brightness and contrast to see if you can create a more exciting composition. Adjusting the brightness and contrast prior to selecting your filter will allow you to make clearer distinctions in your pattern where things seem to blend together.

If an area consistently blends into another, it's often easier to adjust that section separately. (In Photoshop, this is done with the lasso tool.) Once a single area is isolated, you can apply any function you want. It is often helpful to make one or another area brighter or darker or increase the contrast so that the filter result is more appealing.

Save and Print

When you are happy with the way your pattern looks, save it for future reference by using the "save a copy" option, which will not alter your original photo. To print, break the larger picture into smaller, page-sized sections (often called the "tiling" function). Print them, then tape them together in the larger pattern.

There are some copy and print retailers that will size and print your patterns for you. I've found a couple of good websites with this option, too. (I like www.block-posters.com.) Retailers' requirements vary, so check their specifications before working with them.

THE CUTOUT FILTER (LEFT)

The cutout filter reduces the hundreds of colors into just a few. The simplified shapes are easier for cutting, which makes this filter one of my favorites.

ORIGINAL PHOTO (BELOW)

ARTISTIC—POSTER EDGES

This is a good guide for where to do thread painting. In Photoshop, I play with the posterization level, but usually find that the lower numbers work better for this purpose.

BRUSHSTROKES— ACCENTED EDGES

This filter will highlight the design elements in the photo for easier definition.

BRUSHSTROKES—INK OUTLINES

This feature will outline the edges of the elements in the photo. Choose a narrow brushstroke width so that you do not lose details.

Creating a Pattern Without a Computer

If you do not have access to a computer, which is the easiest way to create a pattern, you can still make art quilts with great success. The principles are the same, you will just achieve them in a different manner.

There are several patterns already done in this book for you to use. They can be scanned or copied and blown up to the size you would like your finished art quilt to be. If you're interested in creating your own patterns, this quick and simple exercise will help you with that process.

The one disadvantage you will have in not using a computer program is that you will not have the simplified "cutout" version of your photo to work from. In this case, you will work from the photo and make the decision based on your own eye as to where the pieces should be cut. The process is the same: You will identify the different value sections in the pattern and translate them into fabric in exactly the same way.

To create a pattern of your own, begin with a full-page print of your photo. This can be done on a commercial copy machine or at a copy shop. Start by enlarging the photo in the copier so that it fills an 8½" x 11" sheet of paper, then cut it into four sections and enlarge each section.

Black and White Copies

To save a little money, black and white copies work fine. You'll be working with value anyway, and will have the original photo as reference for color.

2 Enlarge your full-page print to the size you want. The easiest way to do this is to physically cut the print into sections, then enlarge it on a photocopier to the size you need. If you want the image to be the equivalent size of four sheets of paper, cut it into equal fourths. Place each of those cut sections into the copier and enlarge to fill an 8½" x 11" sheet of paper (but leave some room for margins). If you want a larger image, simply begin by cutting the first full-sheet image into more sections and enlarging each into a full sheet.

   Alternate trimming the inside margins on the sections.

3 Put your pattern together, taping the trimmed blocks over the untrimmed blocks. Once the pattern is securely taped together, you're ready to start working.

BLUE BOTTLE 9"x 14"

Chapter Three

BUILDING A
FABRIC COLLAGE

The most important step in creating your art quilt is the fabric collage. The pattern
you have created is just a start to the creative challenges ahead. You can bring
your work to another level by using different patterns and colors to increase the
complexity or re-interpret the photo's composition. You want to make an artwork
that is not just a photo, but represents your vision of the photo.

Choosing fabric is key to interpreting your vision, and here is where you apply
your knowledge of color and value. The same pattern can look entirely different
if fabric choices vary, and for that reason, it is important to try lots of options
before deciding what you like best.

Once your fabrics are selected, you have other options as to how you cut out
your pieces and the way you hold everything together before you sew. In this
chapter, you will be presented with those options so that you can begin to
develop the working style that best suits you.

CHOOSING **FABRICS** FOR YOUR ART QUILT

Once you have prepared the photo that you will be using for your art quilt, the next decision is the colors and fabrics. Do you plan to use colors that are similar to those in the actual photo, or do you want to change some colors, or even the overall tone of the quilt? What is the mood you want to create? Is your subject happy or somber? Is the mood misty and restful or sunlit and full of energy? These questions will help you decide what fabrics to start looking at in order to make your selections.

Once the color itself has been determined, the real work is in finding the fabric values within that color choice. This is very hard to do by eye alone, and where a red viewer makes work much easier. There are many fabrics that appear slightly different to the naked eye, but when viewed through the red viewer will appear exactly the same. The red viewer is always right. If you choose to ignore its "advice" and use those fabrics that look differ-

ent to the naked eye, as soon as you step back a few feet from your finished art quilt, you will see that everything blends together and looks like one fabric. That can be very disheartening after putting so much work into your piece. That is why determining the relative value of your fabric selections is so important. Remember that you need light, medium and dark values, and that the color temperature and saturation all affect the final outcome. Take the necessary time to carefully explore your options before starting. Be sure to select a variety of patterns or textures. The combination of prints, batiks and fabrics that seem to have a texture will create a lively surface design that draws the viewer in. And don't forget to look at the backs of your fabric—sometimes the lighter back is just right for what you need.

COLOR SETS THE MOOD

I was drawn to an old photograph of a stranger because her face was so full of sadness. She became part of a series of portraits I did in shades of different colors to help express the personalities I perceived.

To have made this art quilt in bright colors, or shades of reds and orange or rosy pinks, would have been contrary to the mood. Though greens aren't typical for portraits, I felt they suited the mood here. I chose green fabrics with lots of yellow in them—rather than bright, saturated greens—in order to heighten the sallow and sickly feeling of this sad face. The mood was set initially by the photo itself, but the color scheme supported and heightened the mood.

PORTRAIT IN GREEN 14" × 12"

SEEING TRUE VALUE

To determine a new fabric's place in the value scale of the other fabrics for that design element, lay the new fabric horizontally over the rest and look through a red viewer. If it's the same value as another contender (like here), decide which fabric you like better and eliminate one.

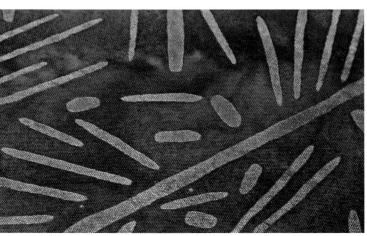

ADD A LITTLE ZING

A zinger is a fabric that is predominantly the right hue and value, but has a lot more going on. Including one or two zingers adds unexpected excitement. Avoid using too many zingers, or the cohesiveness of your quilt will fall apart.

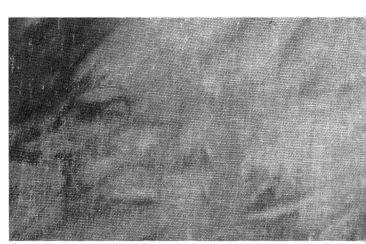

BATIK

One of the beautiful things about commercial batik fabrics is that they have lighter and darker areas of the same color, or a variety of colors. Very often, I take advantage of this light/dark on the surface and "fussy cut" out areas that have the shadow or highlight already there.

WHAT THE QUILT WANTS

What they say about traditional quilts—"Buy the fabric the quilt wants, not the one you want."— is true for art quilts as well. Use the fabric that works, even if it isn't necessarily your favorite. I find this fabric unappealing by itself, but when used in the right settings, it's perfect.

Understanding Value

As discussed earlier, value is at least as important as color alone, and maybe even more important for a successful art quilt. Faces are a good way to learn about value, as I find my students often run into the most trouble working with value while trying to find skin tones.

Gauging the values of skin tones can be daunting because beige fabrics that look different to the eye are often too close in value to be effective.

1 Using the pattern on page 110, we can work on the lovely face inspired by Girl With a Pearl Earring *by Jan Vermeer. Using the cutout filter in Adobe Photoshop, I identified five different values of the skin tones. It doesn't matter if you are working from a color or black and white version of this pattern, value does not change.*

2 Choosing a variety of fabric options, I begin to compare them to the values in the pattern. Looking at the swatches through a red viewer will make it easier to determine which fabrics are closer to the values on the pattern. I also look at the fabrics I have chosen to be sure that they graduate from light to dark, as seen through the red viewer.

EXAMPLE 1

The fabrics in this example all look different to my naked eye, but when used together there is not enough variation in value for them to be really distinguished from each other. All that work, and your finished portrait could end up looking as if it is all made from a single fabric. Up close, you may see the difference, but from even a slight distance, the distinction is lost and the resulting face looks pale and flat.

EXAMPLE 2

Here, there are much clearer differences in the values of the fabrics used. Now you can see the shadows and contours in the face. But the pinkish fabric (which is correct in its value) is too different in hue from the rest and looks like a skin disorder. And although the fabrics graduate from light to dark in value, they are not in sync with the values on the pattern.

EXAMPLE 3

Finally, in this face you can see the balance between color and value. The colors move from light to dark, and nothing looks out of place. The values not only move from light to dark, but each one matches the corresponding value in the pattern.

Again, it is important to trust your eye, not your brain. The whole point of working from a photo is that you only have to see what is there in order to know what to do. A face isn't all one color, nor is it all beige. Look at the shadow areas in this face—taupe, brown, grey. There are lots of colors here that your brain would question. But if the pattern looks right, following it will result in an art quilt that looks right as well.

CUTTING YOUR FABRIC PIECES

Once you have your pattern enlarged to the size of your finished art quilt, trace the main elements onto a piece of Do-Sew that is cut the size of your pattern. This Do-Sew will serve as the foundation for your quilt top. No need to trace every detail; you just want to register the major elements so that their placement is clear.

Whether you're working on your design wall or one element at a time on a table, the process is essentially the same. After making the Do-Sew foundation, trace the pattern to create a template. I usually make several smaller templates, one for each major element of the design. Then you will trace smaller indivdual pieces to cut out of fabric.

Freezer Paper

Freezer paper is a wonderful tool for tracing and cutting out the pieces of fabric that make up your fabric collage. This is the same freezer paper that comes on a roll and is sold in the supermarket. The advantage of freezer paper is that the cutting is easily accomplished without the fabric slipping around. However, it often requires moving back and forth to a window or light box, and it is harder to see through the paper in order to fussy cut a particular area of the fabric. It's the best way, however, to cut small or intricate pieces.

Tracing Paper

Tracing paper or Golden Threads Quilting Paper is another good way to transfer the shapes of each piece from your pattern to your fabric. Since it is easy to see through tracing paper, a light box or window is often unnecessary, and it is easy to see the fabric in order to fussy cut a particular area.

If your section is larger than the piece of tracing paper, tape two pieces together. The disadvantage is that once the tracing is made, the paper must be pinned to the fabric in order to cut out the piece. This is not as secure as the freezer paper, and it is harder to get an accurate cut.

Personally, I prefer to work with tracing paper, partially because I don't worry if the pieces match the pattern exactly. I often eyeball the piece and cut an approximation without tracing at all. The decision to cut the pieces accurately or approximately depends on whether you want to copy the pattern exactly or use it more loosely as a guide.

CREATE A TEMPLATE

It's helpful to create a template of each section you build of your art quilt, in this case the face. This template is a tracing of the pattern and can be placed over your work as it progresses to ensure that all the pieces are in the right location. Each time you add another piece of fabric, lay the template over your work and gently nudge the piece into the corresponding part of the tracing.

54

Tracing Paper or Freezer Paper

You can use either freezer paper or tracing paper to cut out each fabric piece. If you have trouble seeing through the freezer paper, you can outline it on your pattern with a black marker, or if that still doesn't make it clear enough, tape your pattern to a window (during the day) and use it as a light box. Freezer paper has a shiny side and a dull paper side. You will be drawing onto the dull paper side of the freezer paper.

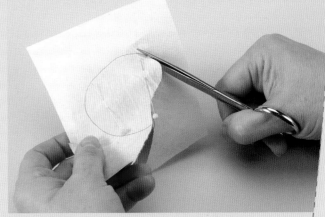

1 If you are using tracing paper, trace the piece you plan to cut, pin it to your fabric and then cut it out.

1 If you're using freezer paper, after tracing your shapes to the freezer paper's dull side, iron the paper (dull side up) to the fabric's right side. Using a warm iron, press the freezer paper onto the fabric and it will adhere to the surface. This makes it very easy to cut around the edges of each shape.

2 Cut around the shape, along the line. Remove the freezer paper from the front and lay the piece onto your work.

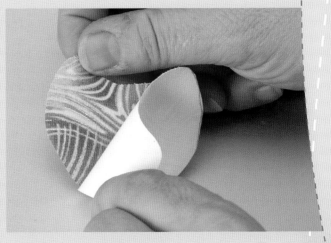

If the iron is too hot when you press your freezer paper onto fabric, it may be difficult to remove. Try scoring the paper with a pin and removing it that way. If it is still too firmly attached, place a damp towel on the freezer paper for a few seconds and then remove it.

NOTES FROM **NANCY**

ATTACHING YOUR FABRIC PIECES

The second thing to consider in deciding how to work on your quilt is how you will attach those fabric pieces to the foundation. You can do this one of two ways: Glue or fusible.

I adhere fabric pieces in place only after I have completed at least a section of the quilt and am sure that it is the way I want it to be. Until I get to that point, I pin the pieces to my design wall so that I can evaluate them as the artwork progresses. Often, I don't do any gluing until the entire piece is pinned and there is nothing else to add—and sometimes I just glue enough to free up some pins when I run out!

Glue

I prefer to work with fabric glue over fusible web because I find it easier and less expensive. Any glue made for fabric is fine, or you can use Elmer's glue diluted with a small amount of water. The many types of fabric glue available in quilt and craft stores will all work well for this technique. Use only a dab of glue here and there to avoid creating lumps or puckering in the surface of the fabric.

When using glue, the whole point is to keep all these little pieces of fabric in place until you can get the quilt to the sewing machine and permanently attach them. You want to use as little glue as possible so that it will be easy to sew over and won't distort or show through your fabric.

Refer to exercise 7 on page 57 for instructions on how to use glue to attach your pieces to the foundation.

Fusible Web

If you prefer the look of collage with edges that do not fray or have any loose threads, then you will want to use a fusible web instead of glue. Fusible web is a glue web that melts under heat. It comes with either one or two sides protected by paper on the roll. There are many brands of fusible web available, but it is important to use one that comes in sheets or by the yard—not the ones that come in ¼" wide rolls, which you would use to do a hem.

The advantage to using fusible web is that the adhesive extends right to the edges of each cut piece so there is no fraying or threads that come loose. If you want a cleaner edge to each piece, this is the way to go. The disadvantage is that you cannot work directly on a design wall, as the foamcore cannot withstand the heat of the iron.

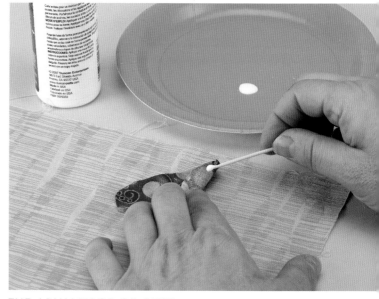

THE ADVANTAGE OF GLUE
Glue is the only way to work if you are doing the piece entirely on a design wall or on a piece of foamcore. When using glue to secure the pieces, you will retain the raw edge look of the fabric in the finished piece.

NOTES FROM **NANCY**

Traditionally, when using a paper-backed fusible web, the mirror image of the design is traced on the paper. In this instance, the paper side of the fusible web product is not used to trace pattern pieces—the product is used only as a fusing agent. After pressing the paper-backed fusible web to the wrong side of the fabric, choose either the tracing paper or freezer paper technique to cut out the pattern. Then, remove the paper backing after the piece is cut out.

Working With Fusible Web

Fusible web can replace glue as the way to hold the pieces together until you are ready to sew. One advantage of fusible web is that it will fuse the entire piece, which means nothing can move around while you sew. It also means that there will be no fraying edges. One disadvantage is that if you are using a design wall foamcore board to build your work, you can't do the pressing required to set the fusible web without removing the quilt, which could jostle pieces. Also, you must attach the fusible web to all the fabrics you plan to use before you cut them out.

NOTES FROM **NANCY**

There are many types of fabric glue available in quilt and craft stores, and they will all work well for this technique. The trick is to use only a dab of glue here and there so that you don't create any lumps or puckering in the fabric surface.

1 *To attach the fusible web to your fabric, remove the paper from one side, or identify the web side (it will feel rough while the paper side will feel smooth). Place the piece of fusible web on the underside of your fabric. Press with an iron (follow the directions for the particular brand of fusible web you are using) to attach the fusible web to the underside of your fabric.*

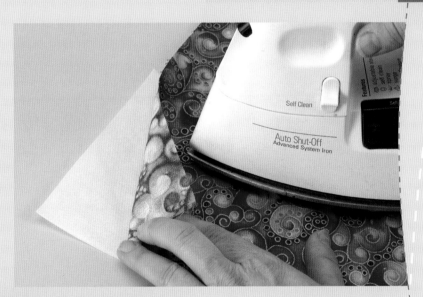

2 *Cut your pieces from the fabric with fusible web on the back. When all of your pieces are in the right position, place a press cloth over the surface.*

If you plan to use freezer paper when cutting out your shapes, leave the paper on the back until the piece is cut; otherwise, you will fuse the fabric to your ironing board! When you have cut out your piece, remove the freezer paper. Using a hot iron, apply heat by pressing up and down, not back and forth. Remove the press cloth and make sure everything is attached.

Creating Your Collage One Element at a Time

For complex art quilts, it's too overwhelming to attempt the entire composition at once. Instead, break the composition into "elements," or small sections that can be completed one at a time and added to the quilt.

For this exercise, you will learn the basics of fabric collage by working on this simple bottle (the background will be addressed in exercise nine on page 62). In this case, it's the only element in the quilt, but it could easily be one of many elements in a more complex quilt. You will find the bottle pattern on page 104. I printed it the size of one sheet of 8½" x 11" paper.

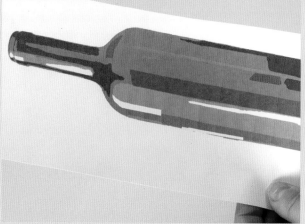

1 Create the pattern and print it. You can print it in color if you're following the colors of the pattern. If you're planning to use other colors, print it in black and white.

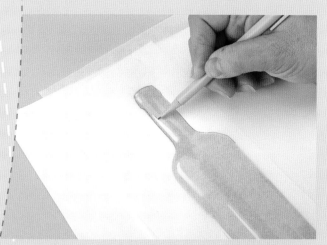

2 Next, create a template. Using a window as your light box if necessary, trace the entire bottle onto tracing paper. If the size you have chosen is larger than a single sheet of tracing paper, tape two or more together.

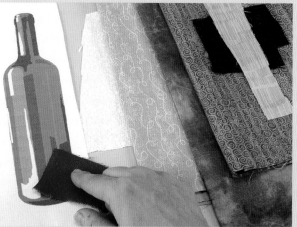

3 Choose your fabrics. Beginning with the blues, select several fabrics and lay them side by side. Use your red viewer to determine their order from light to dark and eliminate any that look the same under the red viewer.

Although you have identified the colors and established a variation of values, you want to be sure they are in the same value range as those in the pattern. Use your red viewer to look at the fabric you have chosen for a particular color next to that color in the pattern. When you have determined which blue fabrics you will use, move on to the magenta.

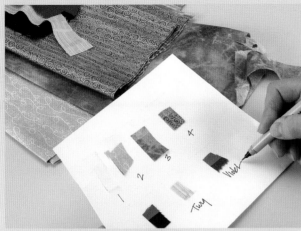

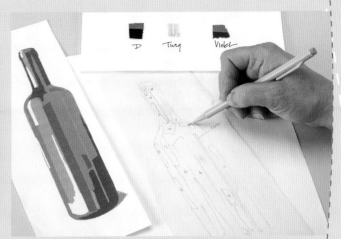

4 Once you have decided which fabrics to use in which order, make a chart so you can number the fabrics. I use a small square of each fabric taped to a sheet of paper, but use whatever type of guide that works for you. A numbered list with a description of the fabric—"the little floral" or "the swirly blue"—will work, too.

5 Refer to the pattern and identify the values by number. You can mark those numbers right on the pattern and/or the template. The lightest value would be "1", the next fabric would be "2", etc. Now you will know which fabric goes in which places.

6 Cut out the foundation piece. In this case, since I'm only doing the bottle, the largest piece becomes the foundation. Identify the fabric you have chosen for that number (you will not be using the fabrics in number order) and trace the shape for that piece onto a second piece of tracing paper or freezer paper. Pin or press this tracing to the fabric and carefully cut out the piece of fabric. Lay this foundation piece on your table top, right side up.

7 Place a piece of tracing paper over the printed pattern and trace the other, smaller pieces of the design element, usually various shapes of color or value.

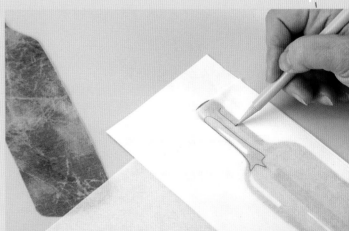

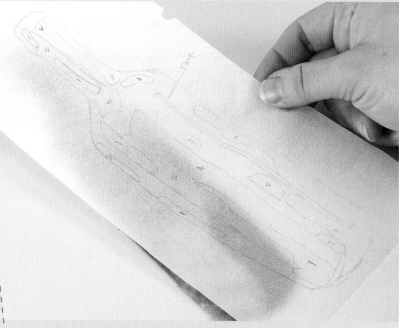

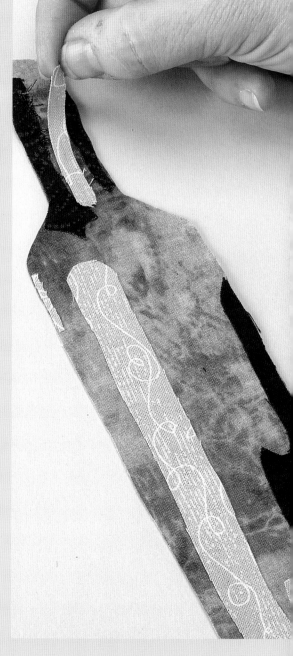

8   *Starting with the darkest values, lay these pieces onto the foundation piece in the approximate place you think they belong. Do not pin them. Take your template tracing and lay it over the top of your work, lining up the edges of the foundation piece. Now you can see exactly where the new pieces should fit. If they need to be moved, gently reach below the tracing paper and use a pin or seam ripper to nudge them into the correct position.*

    Where one piece sits along side another, it is always better to cut one of them a bit larger and layer the other over it. Pieces that butt up to each other rather than overlap tend to move and leave spaces when the quilt is being sewn together.

9   *Move on to the next color, placing the pieces as you see them on the pattern and checking with the template overlay.*

    Where one piece sits along side another, it is always better to cut one of them a bit larger and layer the smaller piece over it. Pieces that butt up to each other rather than overlap tend to shift when the quilt is being sewn together.

NOTES FROM **NANCY**

At this stage, it's not too late to change a fabric. If you feel that a color value is too intense or weak, cut a lesser or greater value in that color and test out the look. Use a pair of binoculars to view your quilt, looking through them from the wrong side! You'll see a concentrated image of your design and be able to tell which fabric selection is the best selection.

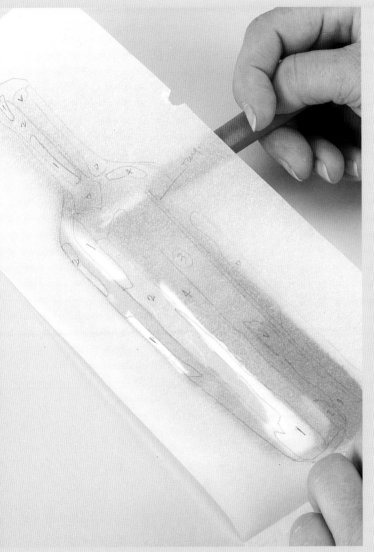

10 Continue placing the pieces, carefully adjusting them with a seam riper or pin. When all the pieces are in place, look at your work and make sure you like the way it looks. Sometimes a single fabric will jump out as wrong; make any adjustments until you are happy with the result. Remember there is no right or wrong; this is your art, so it's your vision.

11 When the pieces are all in the proper place, secure them with glue. Squeeze a small amount of glue onto a disposable plastic plate. The glue hardens quickly, so work with a small amount, replenishing as needed. (Fabric glue is best for this step, but Elmer's glue works well if diluted with a bit of water.)

To apply glue, hold the piece in place with a pin or your finger. Dab a toothpick in the glue, then slide the toothpick underneath the fabric to apply the glue. Use just enough to hold the fabric in place. The less glue you use, the better off you will be later.

When the glue dries, place a press cloth over the piece and gently press so that everything is nice and flat. Because the glue is only temporary, you'll need to stitch these pieces down once you've finalized your composition.

Use Your Eyes, Not Your Brain

When working on an art quilt, my brain will often tell me that a certain area should be different than it appears on the pattern. But, because it comes straight from a photo, the pattern is always right. It's okay to simplify and eliminate some parts or change colors, but trust what you see on the pattern in terms of relationships, perspective and shadows.

Choosing a Background Color

Whether it is a simple or complex art quilt, once the basic design elements are complete, I explore options for the background before making a final commitment. There are two things to think about: the color and the pattern. How these relate to the other fabrics in your quilt can have very different results. Usually, I pin different fabrics to my design wall, pin the design elements on top, step back and analyze. It can also be helpful to take a digital photo of each option so that they can be easily compared

NOTES FROM NANCY

I like to think of this section as **auditioning**! When selecting background colors, consider getting reactions from family or friends—whose taste you respect! My son, Tom, is my in-house art critic. He helps me make decisions in mere seconds. I value his knee-jerk reactions to background and border choices!

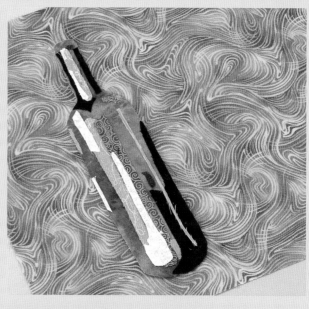

FIRST POSSIBILITY

Orange is the complementary color of blue, so using an orange background will create a lot of life in the art quilt. But in this case, the orange is so strong that it overpowers the blue bottle and takes center stage.

SECOND POSSIBILITY

I like the idea of the magenta which is used in only a tiny piece on the bottle. The dark value makes the bottle stand out.

THIRD POSSIBILITY

This light blue is also used in the bottle and works well for that reason. But it is not very exciting.

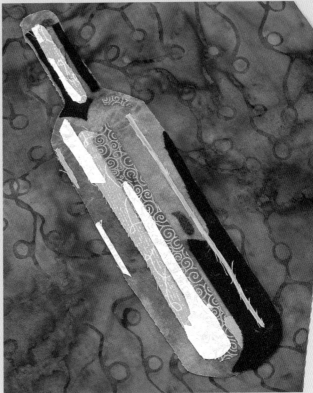

FOURTH POSSIBILITY

The dark background (above) is good for most of the bottle, but blends in too much where the dark shadow is located on the edge of the bottle. The fabric is plain and uninteresting.

FIFTH POSSIBILITY

I like this fabric (above right); it's dark enough to set off the lighter bottle, and there is a bit of orange that does not overwhelm the blue in the bottle. There are areas of blue which relate to the bottle color, and the swirly pattern is interesting without taking over. When using a fabric like this, the placement of the bottle onto the fabric can make a big difference.

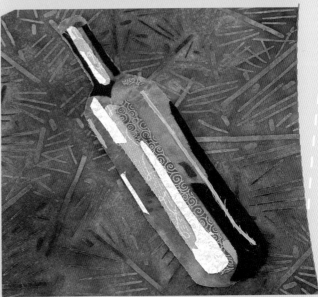

SIXTH POSSIBILITY

The orange in this fabric (above) does not overwhelm the blue, but the green in this fabric does not relate to the other colors and therefore doesn't add anything positive.

SEVENTH POSSIBILITY

In this case (left), I like the dark blue except that it is too close to the dark areas of the bottle, which makes the bottle blend into the background. The additional green in the fabric does not add anything in particular, but as it is a subtle blend, it isn't a real negative.

Deciding on a Composition

Using the same blue bottle, and having decided on the colors that best compliment it, let us examine different compositions and discuss them:

HORIZON LINE—HIGH
In this example, the darker fabric occupies ⅔ of the background space, making it the dominant color and leaving only ⅓ of the "air space" at the top of the composition.

HORIZON LINE—LOW
The opposite is true, here. The darker fabric is only ⅓ of the space now and looks more like the bottle is sitting on a table top.

HORIZONTAL + VERTICAL
Although the ⅓ dark and ⅔ light in the background work well, adding another ⅓ piece to one side makes the composition more complex, and complements the height of the bottle. This will also allow me to add another color—like that orange that was so overwhelming in a larger piece.

HORIZON LINE—DIAGONAL
Remember that diagonal lines make a composition more dynamic, so here, I angled the "table top" where it meets the side. Whereas the horizontal lines were static, this is more exciting.

ANALYZING THE COMPOSITION

This is the final composition I chose, and why.

The background color worked well because it contained a lot of orange (blue's complement), but also had blue lines in it, which coordinated with the blue in the bottle. This fabric had some darker areas and lighter areas, so I had to "fussy cut" it. Because there are light highlights on the left side of the bottle, that tells me that the light source is coming from the left. I wanted to remain true to the light source, so I made sure the brighter orange was on the left and the color moved into the darker, bluer tones on the right. This serves to function as the light and shadow in the background.

I decided to break up the background to create $1/3 : 2/3$ ratio. I chose the lighter, brighter turquoise for several reasons: The blueness complements the muted orange; it is light in value, which works with the light source coming from the left, and makes the highlights in the bottle more naturalistic; a small strip of the same fabric is featured in the bottle, which helps tie the subject to the background.

Instead of putting in a straight horizon line in the form of a table top, I angled it. Angled lines are more dynamic than straight lines, and that is a nice contrast to the straight line of the bottle itself, as well as the strong vertical line of the background.

The deep purple for the table top was also a conscious decision. This particular fabric has some violet undertones, which I thought related nicely to the touch of violet in the bottle. (I tried the violet fabric, but the value was too close to the background and it disappeared). The deep color provided the contrast to make everything work well together.

Finally, I added the touch of shadow to the table top under the bottle (actually a piece of the bluer part of the background fabric). This strengthens the impression of the light source and helps to ground the bottle in the environment, while providing visual separation between the dark blue of the bottle and the dark purple of the table top.

BLUE BOTTLE 9" × 14"

Building More Complex Art Quilts

Now that you have done a very simple art quilt of the bottle, it is time to use that knowledge to complete art quilts of an entire photograph. It is easiest to start with simple photos without too many small pieces and little details and then move on to more difficult art quilts as you become comfortable with the process.

Use Your Design Wall

If you have a design wall, pin the Do-Sew foundation to the wall so that each element can be added as you complete it. Otherwise, pin the Do-Sew to a piece of foamcore to use as your portable design wall.

REFERENCE PHOTO

I love this photo. Even from the back, we can see the girl's intensity as she watches the dolphin come close. The boy's hand, placed on the glass as if trying to touch the dolphin, provides a link between them.

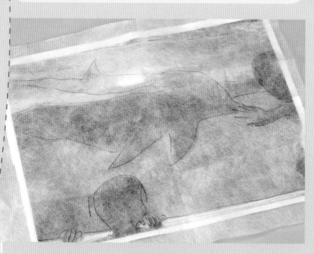

1 *Begin by placing a piece of Do-Sew over your pattern and tracing the main elements onto the Do-Sew with a permanent marker (be sure to use a permanent marker so that there is no chance ink will run onto your fabric). Don't worry about transferring every little detail; you just want to know where each finished element will rest. This is your quilt top base.*

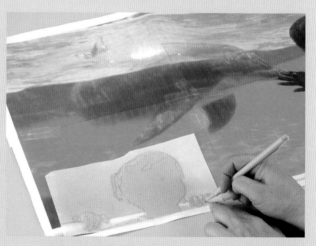

2 *Divide your pattern into a series of smaller elements. There are no rules about what comprises an element; it is a section of the quilt that you determine will be easy to work on so that the quilt is built one piece at a time. Simply break up the photograph into manageable pieces. Make a separate Do-Sew foundation for each element. In this case, the little girl, the little boy and the different parts of the dolphin are each an element on its own foundation piece. Once these are created, make tracing paper templates from the reference photo (as you did for the blue bottle earlier), identifying and cutting out the fabric shapes.*

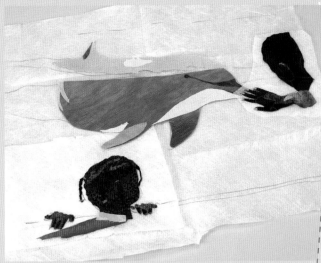

3   Treating each element like the bottle exercise, start with a single element, like the little girl. Lay down the largest piece onto a small piece of Do-Sew and continue to add other pieces one at a time, using the tracing paper template to check on their position. When you are satisfied with the placement of each piece, glue this element together. Now it is ready to pin onto your larger quilt foundation, lined up with the corresponding markings you made from your pattern.

4   As you add each successive element to the art quilt, step back and evaluate. Use a reducing glass or look through a pair of binoculars backward (to reduce rather than enlarge) to see how the composition is coming together. If you are using a "portable" design wall, place it somewhere that allows you to step far back from it and view your emerging art work. A digital snapshot of the quilt viewed on the computer screen can also make it easy to see things you may wish to change.

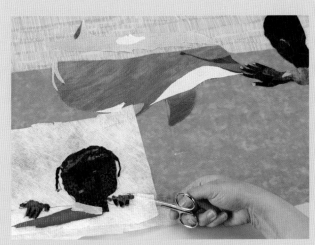

5   Now that all the elements are complete, add the background behind them.

     Trim around each element, so that the Do-Sew is still on the back and holding everything together but doesn't show. This can then be placed onto the background in one (or sometimes more than one) piece. It will also allow you to place your work onto different backgrounds so that you can decide which one you like the best. A digital photo of each potential background makes it easy to compare one to another.

6   Lay in any additional details on the background, and glue everything in place when you're satisfied. Cover with a press cloth, press it flat, and then layer it onto batting. Using a white bobbin thread and a clear, or "smoke," monofilament (colorless) thread, sew the pieces in place using free-motion stitching around their edges. Be sure that each piece is sewn down to the batting.

     The next step will be to thread paint any accents or details (covered in the next chapter), before adding the backing and quilting it all together using clear thread.

Chapter Four

SEWING IT ALL TOGETHER

Now that your fabric collage is complete, it must be sewn together, after which you can add finer detail with thread. Although the decision to add detail is up to you as the artist, you may find that some details are simply too small or delicate to add in fabric pieces. Thread painting is beautiful on its own, but also can be a wonderful way to add texture and detail to a fabric collage.

I identify the thread painting into two categories: direct thread painting and thread-painted appliqué. Both are easy to do, but one or the other is sometimes better for particular situations. The addition of thread work can be just the thing to bring your art quilt to a new level of excitement.

But first, you will need to finish your quilt. This chapter will present you with several ways to do that.

SEWING THE COLLAGE IN PLACE

Once the fabric collage is complete, it must be sewn in place. Neither fusible web nor fabric glue is permanent, so it's essential that all the pieces of your collage be sewn down.

I prefer to do the functional sewing and the ultimate quilting in two separate steps. At this stage I do the functional sewing. I carefully place my glued (or fused) art quilt top onto a layer of batting. Like traditional quilts, all art quilters have a favorite batting—whether it is cotton, poly or a blend—and a preferred weight. I do recommend a fairly thin batting (like traditional weight) so that your quilt top remains flat.

After pressing the quilt top, layer it onto batting and pin with straight pins just enough to hold the top and the batting together.

Unless you specifically want to add a color to the edges of your pieces, your best thread choice for this purpose is monofilament. Monofilament is a clear thread that will disappear and not add any color to your work. This thread has come a long way from what felt like fishing line when it was first introduced years ago. It is now very fine and flexible and usually comes in two "colors"—clear and smoke.

Clear monofilament thread is the right choice for most of your functional sewing. It will disappear on most fabric colors. But on very dark colors, it can be reflective. To avoid reflection, use smoke monofilament. Although using smoke on lighter colors looks grey, on dark colors it disappears completely.

I set my machine for free-motion stitching—darning foot on and the feed dogs dropped. This way I can just follow along the edges of all the pieces of my art quilt, moving forward, backward and side-to-side without having to lift the foot and pivot the fabric. I prefer to use white thread in the bobbin, so that it blends in with the white batting. If you find that the white comes to the surface on very dark fabrics, you may want to change the bobbin color. Because the feed dogs are down, there is no need to worry about sewing with only batting on the bottom. It slides along quite nicely.

Once the functional sewing is complete, press the quilt top again. Now you are ready to add thread-painted accents, if you like.

JUST WALK BY   28" × 22"

Thread Care

Thread naturally deteriorates over time, and more quickly if exposed to light. To test a thread to see if it can still be used, unwind about eight inches and tug. If it breaks easily in your hand, it will certainly break when running through the sewing machine tension at high speed. Any thread on a wooden spool is a lovely memento of days gone by, but it's probably too old to use. Trying to use an old thread will make any project more time-consuming and frustrating.

SELECTING THREADS FOR THREAD PAINTING

Any thread designed for machine sewing will work well for basic construction. For thread painting, different threads will render different effects; thread serves as a palette of paints. A wide selection on hand will ensure you'll have what you want when you need it.

Cotton Thread

Cotton threads will lay down color that is relatively flat and uninteresting. This may not be the best choice for thread painting.

Polyester Thread

Polyester threads have more sheen and therefore more surface interest than those that are 100 percent cotton. They are also recommended for use in the bobbin, regardless of the thread being used on top of the machine, as they produce less lint.

Dual Duty Thread

Dual duty thread with a cotton wrapped polyester core, like Coats and Clark, will give the strength and durability of cotton with the shine of polyester. It is slightly thicker than most polyester thread, comes in many colors, and is relatively inexpensive. Widely available, and appropriate for all types of sewing and quilting, it is also available in small spools, making it easy to purchase lots of colors. Dual duty is also a good choice as a bobbin thread.

Rayon Thread

Rayon threads come in different thicknesses and have a beautiful shine. Rayon thread may not be as colorfast as polyester or cotton threads, and it is not as strong. Rayon threads can be used only as decorative surface threads; they will not hold up for construction.

Trilobal Polyester Thread

Trilobal polyester thread is strong, colorfast and has even more sheen than regular polyester, which makes it a very interesting choice for thread painting. Although it looks like rayon thread, trilobal threads are washable and more durable than rayon.

Metallic Thread

Metallic threads are wonderful for adding a bit of sparkle, but they require a metallic needle on your machine. Metallics now come in a wide range of beautiful colors from a wide variety of manufacturers. A little goes a long way: Metallics are most effective when used in small amounts as an accent.

Glitter Thread

Glitter threads don't look significantly different from metallics on the spool, but the result is vastly different. Often called hologram or holographic threads, glitter threads are translucent and iridescent. They can be washed and ironed under low heat. Like metallic threads, a little glitter thread goes a long way.

Monofilament Thread

Monofilament threads are intended to be used for invisible stitches in quilting. Clear, colorless threads are available for use with most fabric colors, but there are also "smoke" (dark gray) threads which are designed to reduce reflection on darker fabrics. Monofilament thread is used to hold the fabric collage pieces together so that no additional color is introduced. For this reason, it is also used for the final quilting.

Variegated Thread

Variegated threads are made up of a series of colors so that they change color at either regular or irregular intervals. These are not recommended for thread painting. They can, however, create interesting effects when used for surface quilting.

DUAL DUTY THREAD

FREE-MOTION STITCHING

When it comes to thread painting or raw edge appliqué for the design elements, I use free-motion stitching so I can move freely in any direction. The first thing you will need is a darning foot. A sewing machine has feed dogs—a jagged-edged piece in the throat plate that pulls fabric through the machine in a nice straight line. For free-motion stitching, or thread painting, the feed dogs are disengaged, either by dropping them below the throat plate or with an additional plate that fits over them. If your machine does not offer either of these options, set your stitch length to 0. Any of these methods will result in the same thing—your machine will simply stitch in place until you move the fabric.

A darning foot is important because any other type of foot holds the fabric down tightly so that the feed dogs can pull it through. For free-motion stitching (or thread painting) the fabric must be loose enough to float along as you move it. You can control the direction of the thread any way you want—to the side, forward, back, around in circles. The goal is to try to maintain a consistent stitch size, and it should look like the size of a standard machine sewing stitch. The good news is that unlike free-motion quilting, your stitch length isn't as critical when thread painting, as you will be moving back and forth filling in an area with thread, so that variations in stitch length will not be obvious.

Your machine tension, even with a machine that self-adjusts, will probably need to be changed. I find that on my machine, any free-motion sewing or thread painting means bringing the tension number down. Play with your machine to see what gives you balanced tension. Remember that this number may change if you use a different thread or different batting. When you determine the right numbers in each situation, write them down in the inside cover of this book so you won't have to figure it out every time you sit down to thread paint.

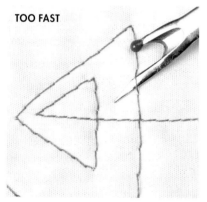

TOO FAST

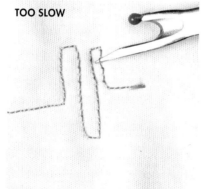

TOO SLOW

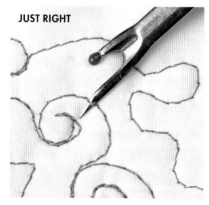

JUST RIGHT

NOTES FROM NANCY

Before stitching, select a needle that is compatible to your thread. A new all-purpose or universal needle is the perfect selection for cotton and polyester threads. When choosing metallic, rayon, or glitter threads, use an embroidery needle or Metafil needle. The eyes of these needles are longer, preventing shredding or fraying of the thread.

LEARNING TO STITCH FREELY

With free-motion stitching, the learning curve is coordinating the speed of the machine and the speed at which you move the fabric. If you move the fabric too quickly, the result will be big loopy stitches. On the other hand, if you move the fabric too slowly, it will result in tiny little dots of thread.

EXERCISE TWELVE
Practicing Free-Motion Stitching

If you've never done free-motion stitching, take a piece of solid colored fabric with batting underneath, drop your feed dogs, put on the darning foot and just start playing. The more you practice, the easier it gets.

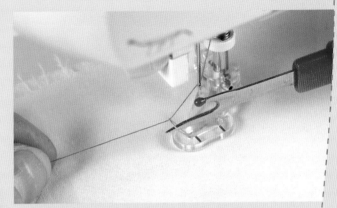

1 For your first attempt, trying stitching on a light or white background with vividly colored thread so you can see your stitches clearly. Change to your darning foot and pull the bobbin thread up to the surface of your fabric so that it doesn't get caught when you stitch in different directions.

2 Start with big, looping stitch designs rather than tight, little ones. The more you practice, the more control you will develop. Lock your stitches at the beginning and end of a line of stitching (easily done by simply stitching in place a few times) so that your stitches don't come out.

3 When you feel comfortable with free-motion stitching, find a fabric that has a large print, like a floral. Match your thread to one of the colors on the fabric and start "coloring in" a section of that color. Use your needle the way you would use a fine point felt tip marker: Fill in with color using little back and forth movements, gradually moving into other areas. Trying to make big, sweeping, back-and-forth motions in a confined area will be harder to control. The more you practice, the more control you will have, and you will find that it won't take long to fill in even the smallest areas like a pro.

THREAD-PAINTED ACCENTS

There are two ways of using thread painting in your art quilts: direct thread work and thread-painted appliqué. Both methods involve a basic variation of free-motion stitching.

Direct thread painting involves thread painting on the quilt itself, either coloring in or outlining. This method is good for detail work on faces, or adding trees and other items that have a lot of background showing through.

Thread-painted appliqué begins with the image printed onto a computer-printable fabric sheet, which is thread painted before it is machine appliquéd onto the quilt. This allows you to try it several ways before adding it to your quilt.

DIRECT THREAD-PAINTED EMBELLISHMENTS
I used direct thread painting to add all the detail on the woman's face in MARKET DAY, SARLAT, and also to fill in areas of her clothing, adding texture and color.

DIRECT THREAD-PAINTED DESIGN ELEMENTS
Because the lamp's filigree is so delicate, it would have been nearly impossible to reconstruct it out of fabric, especially at that size. With thread painting, I was able to add this detail to MARKET DAY, SARLAT.

THREAD PAINTING TO "COLOR"

The painting of the face (right) is direct; a classic "coloring" approach. The direct thread painting added texture to An Outstreched Hand, defined the face and emphasized the hues and values where needed.

THREAD PAINTING APPLIQUÉ

The figure in Life Was Simpler When All I Needed Was Teddy (left) is thread-painted appliqué. I printed this photo onto printable fabric, added the thread painting details, like the hair, then cut the figure out and sewed it to the quilt.

THREAD PAINTING APPLIQUÉ AND DETAIL

These figures in Museum Steps are also thread-appliquéd. The thread painting on the figures adds detail, such as the stripes in the orange shirt and the dark threads in the folds of the clothing to suggest shadow.

Direct Thread Painting

There are many instances when thread painting is the best way to achieve a level of detail that would be difficult using fabric pieces alone. In the case of this piece, SEASCAPE (pattern on page 114), the tree is an important element. I love how delicate it looks in the photo, especially when compared with the roughness of the rocks. If done in fabric, it would lack fine detail, so I decided to do it in thread.

You don't need to make this art quilt in order to practice thread painting the tree. Try it on a piece of scrap fabric and practice until you get the hang of it. The process is the same whether it is a tree, a face or any other detail being done in thread.

Prevent Puckering

A hoop or a piece of paper underneath the quilt will keep it from puckering. If using paper underneath, be sure to remove anything that isn't sewn down when your thread painting is complete; the rest remains in the quilt.

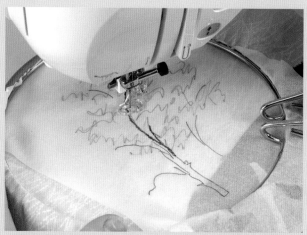

1 *Once the fabric collage is complete, layered over batting and pinned, decide what area you wish to begin your thread painting. Then make a tracing of it from your pattern (either onto tracing paper or Golden Threads Quilting Paper). This tracing does not need to be exact—just the basic shape of the tree trunk and some of the outer edges of the leaves. Pin this tracing to your quilt, then stabilize the area with a hoop. You won't be using the hoop as you do when hand-embroidering. Instead, place the bottom of the hoop on the table, put your quilt area over that and then put on the top part of the hoop. This allows your fabric to sit flat on the bed of the sewing machine.*

2 *With the feed dogs down and the darning foot on, begin with a brown thread for the tree trunk. Using free-motion stitching, trace along the outside edges of the trunk and over the main branches. Don't be too worried about following the lines exactly; no 2 trees are exactly the same.*

When the basic shape of the tree is traced in thread, use the lighter green thread to mark the outermost area of the leaves with little stitch points. Don't connect these; just pull a jump thread between them. Again, remember that accuracy is not important.

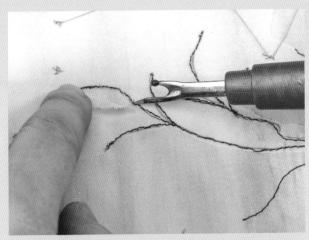

3 Remove the quilt from the sewing machine and score the sewn lines with the dull side of a seam ripper tip. Carefully remove all the tracing paper from the top of your fabric. Cut all the jump threads on both the top and underside of your work.

4 Now that you have the basic outlines of your thread painting on the quilt, return the quilt to the sewing machine to fill in some areas and do more thread painting in others. Using an up and down motion, fill in the trunk of the tree with the brown thread. It doesn't need to be densely filled with thread; little bits of other colors coming through will make it look more natural.

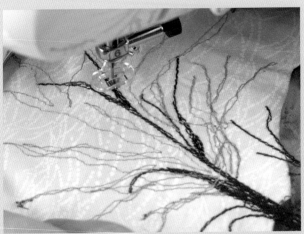

5 Moving back to the green thread, connect those "points" to the central section of the tree. Try to avoid overly straight lines. Relax and have fun with it; there is no right and wrong. Refer to the photo for guidance if necessary.

6 Choose a deeper green thread to add more to the leaves. Using a small circular, free-motion stitch, fill in the areas around the center of the tree with the darker color, radiating out into the branches.

Remove the quilt from the hoop. If there are little wrinkles between the areas of leaves, place the quilt face down on a terry towel and press from the back. Flip it to the top and press gently, using a press cloth to protect your thread work.

Thread-Painted Appliqué

For more intricate thread paintings (like the people on the stairs in MUSEUM STEPS on page 75), a thread-painted appliqué method can be employed. This means that the image is printed onto computer-printable fabric and thread-painted before being added to the quilt. The advantage of this method is that you can try the thread painting a few different times before adding it to your quilt, so that any mistakes are not on your beautiful artwork.

Tip

When using printable fabric, it isn't necessary to print using a "best" setting; it will only lay down more ink than the fabric can absorb. "Draft" mode works fine.

1 Print the image onto fabric in the exact size it will appear on the quilt. (I used the same enlargement of the photo that I used for my pattern. I tried to fit multiple images on a single sheet so I could experiment and choose the best.) Peel the paper off the back and follow the instructions for the particular brand of fabric you are using.

2 Press the fabric sheet and then do a rough cut around the image, leaving at least ¼" around the edges. You can thread paint with or without batting underneath—it's your choice. Batting will add a bit more loft to the image, but it will be added to a quilt with batting. Either way, because this is a fairly small piece, back it with paper before beginning any thread work, or use a hoop.

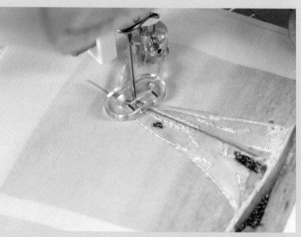

3 Thread paint the image, following the existing colors and doing as much or as little as you think appropriate. This is an artistic decision, and there is no right or wrong way.

4 When you have completed your thread painting, tear away any paper not sewn in. Press and then carefully trim just to its edges.

5 Using either fusible web or a dab of fabric glue, attach the appliqué to your art quilt in its proper place. Fusing or gluing is preferable to pinning as the pins will distort the small thread painting.

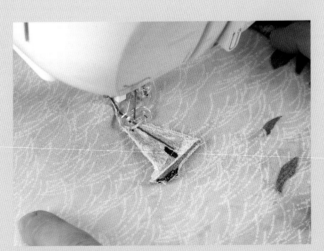

6 Using monofilament thread and free-motion stitching, sew the thread-painted appliqué to the quilt.

7 Stitch over the surface of your appliqué with clear thread to add dimension where you want it.

ADDING **BORDERS** TO YOUR ART QUILT

For the most part, I don't care for borders on art quilts. It is just my opinion, but I think it makes the quilt less "artsy" and more "quilty." But there are exceptions, and I have used borders on some of my quilts.

I usually opt for adding borders when I face one of several problems with my finished piece: It looks too narrow or small; something about the quilt seems out of proportion; there is too much going on in the quilt, and the eye needs a rest; or it simply looks unfinished.

TO BORDER OR NOT TO BORDER?

Usually the decision to border a quilt is because the quilt looks unfinished. Often it is a small quilt that looks as if it needs to end somewhere. This was the case with THE STAIRS. When the thread work was completed and I stepped back to look at it, the narrowness of the piece was out of proportion and it looked too small and insignificant. So I decided to add a border.

THE STAIRS   14" x 21½"

The decision to add a border is just the beginning. What color, what fabric and how wide are the next questions you will need to ask yourself. Auditioning different possibilities is the best way to decide.

Take the Flamingo quilt we used for the example of combining photos. This piece is okay without a border, but the water looks as if it just falls off the two sides. A border will give it a place to end. Try several different options before coming to a decision on your border. Just remember that whatever color you choose for the border will accentuate that color in the quilt.

TESTING A NEUTRAL GRAY
The gray fabric (above) that was used sparingly in the water and shadow areas creates a more neutral frame that complements the quilt without fighting it.

USING FLORAL PINK
Using a pink border (left) will make the flamingos more prominent by drawing attention to that color. But this floral fabric is too strong and becomes the focal point.

TRYING A DIFFERENT PINK
This pink fabric (bottom left) is okay, but personally I think it makes the quilt too "pretty."

A COLORFUL ALTERNATIVE
Finally, I found this blue and green fabric (below) in my stash. It does not appear in the quilt at all. But the green picked up nicely on the green in the water (which is a solid and would have been a boring border), and the blue in the pattern relates to the blue in the water. The pattern itself is reminiscent of water, so this is the one that I like the best.

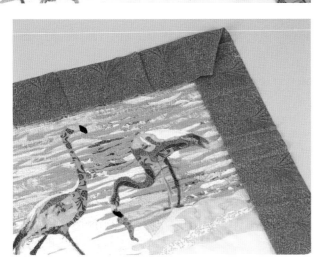

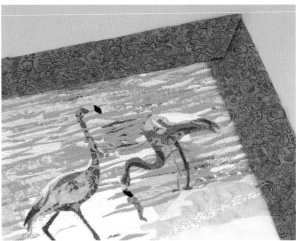

Adding a Border and Border Batting

Most often, the decision to add a border comes after the quilt is finished; and as you have already added the batting, you need to add more under the borders. As you'll see in this exercise, this is easily accomplished:

Whichever fabric you decide to use, remember that the size of the border should be proportionate to the size of the quilt. Using a border that is as wide as ⅓ or ½ the quilt would overpower the artwork.

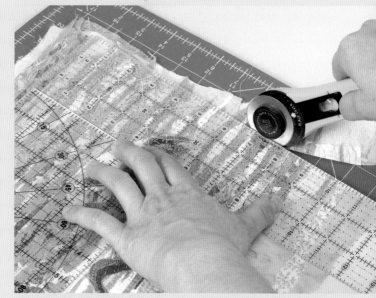

1 *Square off your quilt, leaving a ¼" seam allowance all around.*

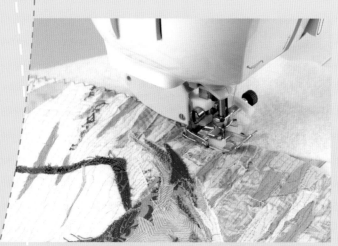

2 *With your rotary cutter, cut batting strips the same width as your borders. Place one batting strip to the right side of the quilt (don't overlap), then attach using a zigzag stitch. Repeat on the left side.*

3 *Lay the right-hand border on the quilt, right sides together. Attach to the quilt with a straight stitch and a ¼" seam. Repeat with left-hand border.*

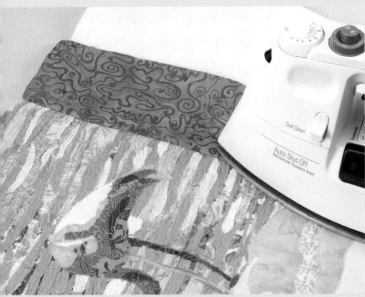

4   *Flip the side borders open and press.*

5   *Place the top batting strip at the top edge of the quilt. Using a wide zigzag stitch, white thread and a walking foot, attach the new batting strip to the quilt. Repeat on the bottom.*
*   Note that the final 2 sides of batting strips will need to be long enough to extend past the left and right edge of the quilt (just as a border does).*

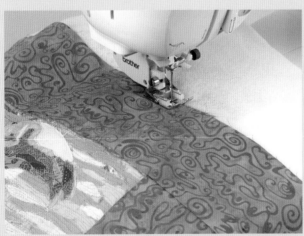

6   *Lay the top border on the quilt, right sides together. Attach it to the quilt with a straight stitch and a ¼" seam. Repeat with the bottom border.*

7   *Press your borders open and square off again. Finish the quilt edges with either a pillowcase edge or binding edge.*

ADDING THE BACKING

I don't add the quilt back until all the work is complete on the quilt top. That means all the collage pieces are sewn in place and any thread painting is finished.

The back can be added in several ways, with different edge finishing options. For a quilt that will have a binding on the edges, I layer the top over the quilt back and do the quilt stitching before adding the binding (exactly as I would for a traditional quilt). For a pillowcase edge, the quilt back is placed face to face with the quilt top, sewn around the edges and turned right side out (check out my technique for making clean edges on page 88), then quilted.

In either case, quilting is a necessary step. Quilting is not decorative (although it can be); it holds the three layers together. Skipping the quilting will cause your art quilt to sag and stretch. Usually, I go over many of the lines I have already stitched with another line of clear thread. You may wonder why I do this twice—why not just let the functional sewing lines hold the pieces in place as my quilting? There is a reason for it: When sewing the collage pieces in place, there are some areas that will be more densely stitched and some areas that are not stitched at all. You may also have bits of tangled thread on the batting side of your work. All of this disappears once you put the back of the quilt over it. Now you can do evenly spaced quilting, and the back of your quilt will look clean and neat.

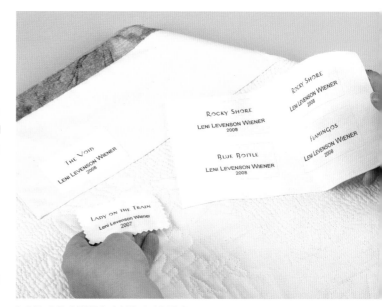

ROD POCKETS AND LABELS

The easiest way to hang your quilt is with a rod pocket. This is placed on the back of the quilt and allows you to slip in either a curtain rod or a wooden dowel with eye hooks at either end to hang on a wall. (The standard size for rod pockets for quilt shows is 4".)

It's also important to label your art quilt with the title, your name and the date completed, plus any other information (such as contact information) you want to include. The label is the only identification your work of art will carry, and it can be as simple or as elaborate as you wish. (I've seen hand-painted and embellished labels that could be works of art themselves.) I like to use computer-printable fabric sheets; this makes the label easy to read and allows me to use interesting fonts from the computer. I wait until I have several to print so that I can do more than one label on a single sheet of fabric.

THE UNBACKED QUILT

Here, you can see how the functional sewing (sewing down the design elements and thread painting) is effectively "quilting" the top and batting. It's best to add the backing after all this thread work, or the back of your quilt would be a busy, thread-covered mess. Adding the backing fabric and then quilting the three layers together creates a clean, neat back to your art quilt (see the back of THE VOID, above).

EDGE FINISHES FOR YOUR QUILT

Finishing an art quilt is no different from finishing any traditional quilt. There are lots of options, and several are featured here.

You may choose to use a binding, a nice finish that allows you to edge the quilt in a particular color or fabric, which becomes a frame for the quilt.

If you do not want to add a frame and want the edges of the art to simply end—then a "pillowcase" finish is the way to go.

Maybe you would prefer to have a free-form shape, or a shape that allows some of the elements of your design to break free of the quilt edge. The finishing method you choose is as individual as your work itself.

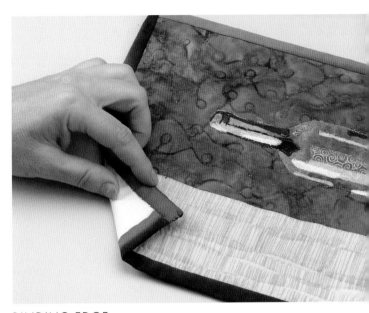

BINDING EDGE
The binding edge will serve as a frame for the composition.

PILLOWCASE EDGE
The pillowcase edge creates a nice, smooth edge that doesn't interfere with the composition. The composition will run to the very edge of the quilt.

FREE-FORM EDGE
Free-form edges allow you to finish the quilt in any shape you want.

Making a Binding Edge

The binding edge can serve as a frame for the composition and also holds up well to wear and tear.

1 *Square off the edge of your art quilt to the size and shape you want. Decide on your binding fabric and cut 4 strips 2½" wide. Press these in half lengthwise with the right side of the fabric on the outside.*

2 *Lay your quilt top over your backing, which is lying right side down. Pin the binding strips to 2 opposite edges of the quilt, with the raw edges lined up with the raw edge of the quilt.*

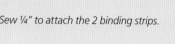

3 *Sew ¼" to attach the 2 binding strips.*

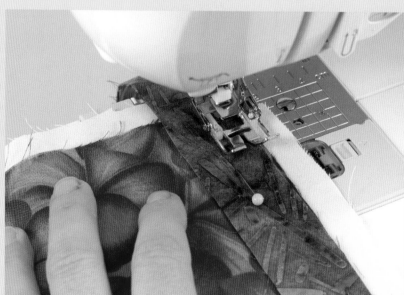

4 Trim the top and bottom edges of the binding strip in line with the quilt. Fold the binding strip to the quilt front and secure either by sewing it or at least pinning it in place (trim the batting edge if necessary so that the binding rolls over to cover the stitch line in the back).

5 Pin the other 2 binding strips to the remaining edges, folding in ½" at the beginning and end for a nice clean corner. Sew ¼" to attach them.

6 Finally, fold these bindings over, then secure all bindings to the back using either a machine or hand stitch.

If you choose to add a rod pocket, simply pin the raw edges of the rod pocket to the raw edges of the top of the quilt back and sew everything together when attaching your binding strip.

NOTES FROM **NANCY**

Creating a Pillowcase Edge

In general, I prefer to finish my art quilts with a pillowcase back without any visible binding around the edge. A pillowcase back means that the quilt front and the quilt back are placed right sides together; the edge is sewn all the way around leaving a small opening through which the quilt will be turned right side out. This opening is then hand-stitched closed. It has

always been my experience that no matter how carefully I hand-sew that opening, it never blends in perfectly with the rest of the edges, so I do my pillowcase backs with one additional step which helps me avoid that problem.

1 Start by squaring off the quilt top. Cut a quilt back that is a few inches larger than the top on all sides. Determine which is the top edge of the quilt back and cut a strip from it about 3" wide.

2 With right sides together, pin this strip to the top edge of the quilt back and sew in from the 2 sides, leaving an opening in the center about 4–5" wide. Press.

3 Place the quilt top and backing right sides together. Pin them in place. Using a walking foot, sew the front to the back with a ¼" seam allowance. Use the quilt top as your guide. Sew all the way around all 4 sides.

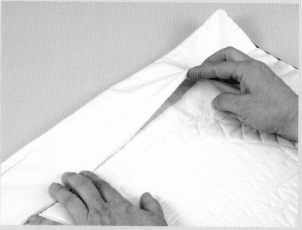

4 Using the opening that was left near the top of the quilt back, turn the quilt right side out and press so that it lays flat. The opening can now be slip-stitched closed and will be covered by the rod pocket.

Finishing a Free-Form Shape

Art quilts don't all need to be squares or rectangles. You may decide that your art quilt would look better with a free-form edge. Free-form edges, however, can be difficult to finish with a binding or pillowcase back. This method does the trick.

If you'd like to have a free-form shape, yet would appreciate seeing what the edge would look like before cutting, use a flexible ruler, bending or shaping until you've found the ideal shape. Mark along the edge of the ruler and then cut.

1 *Pin the quilt back to the back of the quilt front, not unlike the way you would begin to do a binding edge.*

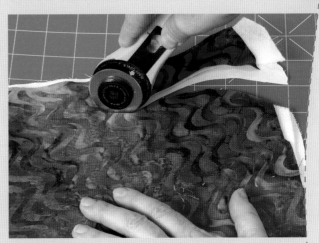

2 *Using a rotary cutter and cutting mat, cut your free-form edges. Add some more pins closer to the edges of the quilt.*

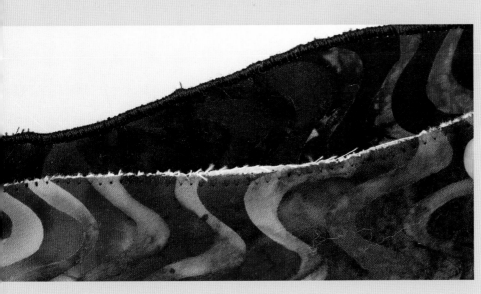

3 *Using a zigzag or satin stitch and a walking foot, sew all the way around the edges of the quilt, lining up the edge of the quilt with the center marking of the foot so that the stitches encase the top, batting and backing. Experiment with scrap fabric to determine how wide or how tight you want your stitches to be, and whether you prefer them done in a colored thread or a clear monofilament thread.*

MOVING BEYOND THE FRAME

Another option often employed in art quilts is to have something break free of the frame. The quilt is still rectangular or square in shape, but one or two elements extend outside of the frame. What breaks free is not a random decision; it is done for impact.

In An Outstretched Hand, the woman's hand, the top of her head and her arm break free of the frame. More subtly, the bag she is carrying also forms the quilt edge not contained in the rectangular shape. The elements that extend out of the frame are those that draw your eye first.

So by extending the hand—the name of the piece and the focus of the picture (she is begging, she isn't just an elderly woman)—it becomes the focal point of the piece.

The same is true of her face. I wanted her face to be at least as important as her hand, so having it extend slightly out of the "box" draws the eye there as well. Finally, the arm, the edge of the bag she is carrying and the hem of her coat are also not contained in the box, which creates immediacy, as if she is moving toward the viewer, heightening the drama.

RUFFLED FEATHERS   31" × 26½"

MOVEMENT

Allowing the head and wings of the goose to move outside the frame of this quilt (above) heightens the sense that he is moving quickly toward the viewer. His opened mouth and forward-moving feet indicate he is in attack mode; breaking free of the quilt edges removes him from the background.

EMOTION

This quilt (left) would not be as dramatic or emotional if the woman was encased in a rectangular quilt. The title, An Outstretched Hand, would not have the same impact if that hand did not extend outside the edge of the quilt.

AN OUTSTRETCHED HAND   21½" × 30"

Working Outside of the Box

If you choose to have design elements extend outside of the box, you can finish the quilt using a combination of the pillowcase back and the free-form finish.

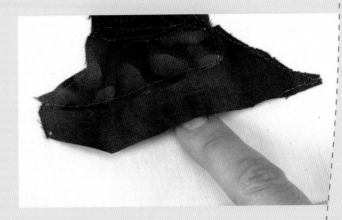

1   Square off the quilt and trim the bottom up to your "jut out" ¼" larger than you want the finished edge (your seam allowance).

2   Sew all around your quilt edge, as you would for any pillowcase-backed quilt, stopping at the edges of the area that juts out of the quilt.

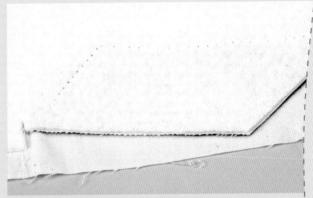

3   At that spot where you stopped stitching, carefully clip to release the edge of the seam allowance.

4   Turn the quilt right side out and press. Make sure that the batting and backing are smooth, with no wrinkles or puckers underneath the part of the quilt that extends beyond the edges. Pin all 3 layers in place and trim the edges so that they all end at the edge of the element that juts out.

5   Using a clear thread and a walking foot, set your machine for a zigzag stitch and encase all 3 layers at the edge. I sew with the center line of the walking foot on the edge of the fabric.

Chapter Five

CREATIVE ADVICE

The information in this book is only a starting point for you, the artist. It is important to remember when reading any book or taking any class that instructors describe the methods they find most helpful. It is important for you to take in all the information you can but then formulate your own way of doing things.

The creation of your art quilt is not the full measure of your artistic expression; naming your quilt, finishing it in a way that looks clean and professional and finding ways to express yourself are all part of the package.

It is my hope that you will use this book as a guide; but that along the way you will go off on your own road, expressing your own personality and creative preferences.

The Endless Dance of the Ponytail 29¼" x 30"

NAMING YOUR ART QUILT

As with any work of art, your art quilt needs a name. Many artists choose to give their quilts fairly straightforward names, like STUDY IN BLUE or COMPOSITION IN SHADES OF GRAY. Some number the names in a series, like ORANGE SQUARES No. 1. I even know art quilters who start with an intriguing title and work from there.

Naming your quilt gives you the opportunity to let the viewer know what it is you want them to see in the artwork, or it can be part of the intrigue that draws them in to look at the piece. Often, the name will evoke a different response from the viewer than you had intended; but this is a good thing, as every person who looks at your art quilt will have a reaction based on their personal life experiences.

Frequently, I have a working title for a piece that changes when I complete it. Often, when looking at the finished art quilt, one aspect or detail of the quilt jumps out at me and consciously may not have been the focus while I was making it.

Choosing a title for your art quilt is as personal as the choice of subject and the choice of fabrics. I find it interesting that when looking for a name for a piece, I get as many suggestions as the number of friends I ask. This is because everyone sees something different in each piece. Choosing a name can help direct the viewer to look for what you hoped to convey.

PATIENCE   29" x 40"

NOTES FROM NANCY

In addition to giving my art quilt a name, I always add my signature to the label and suggest you do the same. After all, you've created an art quilt!

PLAY ON WORDS

The art quilt PATIENCE was called SHE WAITS throughout the time I was working on it. But "patience" had a double entendre. This art quilt started with a photo of a woman sitting next to one of the huge granite lions in front of the New York Public Library in New York City. The two famous lions are named "Patience" and "Fortitude." It happened that the lady waiting for someone was sitting next to "Patience." I liked the play on the word—the lion is patient and she clearly is not: Her body language says she is anxious and impatient.

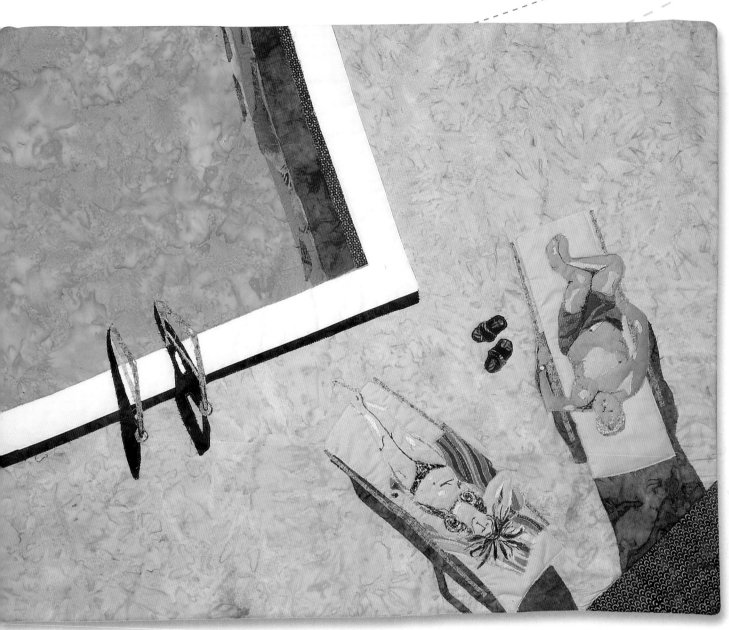

LIGHTLY TOASTED 28" × 22"

BY ANY OTHER NAME

It wasn't until this quilt was complete that I noticed that the man resembled
Bill Clinton. The lady, however, looks nothing like Hillary Clinton. Although
I wanted to call this quilt BILL BUT NOT HILLARY, I didn't want anyone to think
I was making a political statement, so I named it LIGHTLY TOASTED (but I have
to admit I still think of it as BILL BUT NOT HILLARY).

WORKING IN A SERIES

Many artists, not just art quilters, prefer to work in a series. A series can be any group of artworks that are related in some way. A series can give the artist an opportunity to explore many aspects of one idea, more than could be expressed in a single piece. Not limited to subject, a series can represent a technique, a color scheme or tell a story, with each piece providing another aspect or viewpoint. Working in a series allows an artist to explore a wide range of ideas that could not all be expressed in a single art quilt, and the result is a group of pieces that work well together.

A series need not be completed at one time. A particular series might be something you come back to time and again to try a different approach, to return to an idea about which you have a new thought or idea. And pieces can overlap into more than one series. Like most other aspects of creating art, there are no rules governing what is a series and what can be included. It is only a "thread" that means something to the artist.

PORTRAIT IN GREEN   14" × 12"

PORTRAIT IN ORANGE   14" × 12"

PORTRAIT IN YELLOW   15" × 12"

PORTRAIT IN BLUE   15" × 12"

FINDING YOUR OWN VOICE

Finding your own voice is an important part of your development as an artist. In the beginning, you will be influenced by the techniques you learn, the teachers whose classes you take, the books you use or the art quilts you see in books and exhibits that you love. But once you begin to branch out, develop your own way of working and your own techniques, you will begin to be comfortable with who you are, working on art quilts that reflect you, not your influences. This confidence is called finding your own voice.

For me, finding my voice was as much a function of what I don't like to do as the things I like to do. Reflecting on the aspects of making an art quilt that I enjoyed and did not enjoy, I made a list. I make art quilts for the pleasure of it and decided that I didn't want to ever say to myself, "Oh, I hate this part." So I stopped doing the things I didn't like. I had little patience for piecing; I wanted to see the art quilt develop quickly and spontaneously, and tedious piecing took that spontaneity away. I also decided I do not like doing bindings, so I don't do them anymore. Conversely, I love thread painting and raw edge appliqué, so they became the focus of my art quilts. You will have different likes and dislikes on your list—that is what makes you a unique individual.

Finding my voice was also a function of the kinds of pieces I make, the subject matter and how I handle that subject matter. You may be inspired and influenced by the beauty of nature—as many artists are. I am not a flower person, although I find trees, rocks and water beautiful. But I prefer to do art quilts with people in them. With few exceptions, the people in my quilts don't even look at the viewer. I like to make quilts that capture a private moment in a person's public life—an inspiration that I am sure comes from my years as a photographer.

Your voice will change. As you change and grow as an artist, your interests and viewpoints will, too. As your technique improves, you will be comfortable tackling art quilts that you might have thought too difficult earlier in your journey. Challenging yourself and moving forward will always have an effect on your viewpoint and execution—your personal voice.

Journal Quilts

Journal quilts have become quite popular recently. Journal quilting is like keeping a diary, but your words are replaced with small art quilts. Because of the smaller dimensions, these can be completed in a day, which can free you up to explore lots of ideas. You can create a journal quilt every day, every few days, once a month—the rules are your own.

Often journal quilts become studies for larger pieces or even a series. Many journal quilters work in a consistent size and sew the quilts together into a book. Whatever you choose to do with them, journal quilts will help you expand and explore your art quilt options.

LADY ON THE TRAIN   32½" × 29½"

ARTIST'S SHORTHANDS: FACES

The following list of tips, or "shorthands," as I like to call them, will help you construct art quilts that focus on the human face (like the Vermeer exercise on page 52).

Faces

When working on a face, it is easiest to work on a table top and add the face to the design wall after it is completed and glued. Start with a base fabric—use the color that is most prominent in the face and cut out the silhouette of the face. This will help provide reference points for placement of your other fabrics. Layer one fabric at a time, as with any other project. For a face to resemble a particular person, subtleties are important. Use the tracing to help position pieces like the eyes and mouth. A slight slant or an eye that is a fraction of an inch off will change the look and make the person less recognizable. Using the tracing as an overlay, these pieces can be positioned so that they provide an accurate resemblance. Always use a true white for the whites of the eyes; this will provide the contrast that makes the face look alive.

Lips

Lips can be done easily using only three fabrics: the base color plus one lighter and one darker. The overall shape of the lips is cut from the base fabric. A smaller piece is cut from each of the two other fabrics—in shapes that are oval. The lighter fabric, placed along the lower part of the mouth, helps give the illusion of fullness. The darker fabric, placed toward the top of the mouth, gives the illusion of the separation of the lips. A little thread to clearly define that separation line finishes the job. Often, I use the back of the lip fabric as the highlight spot, a great match of color in a lighter value.

Eyes

The trick to doing a convincing eye in fabric is to use a white fabric and a very dark fabric. If the whites of the eyes are not true white, or the fabrics lack contrast, the eye won't be as successful. The reflective dot in the eye (use your photo as a guide) gives the eye life. Details can be added in thread to finish.

PORTRAIT IN ORANGE   14" x 12"

WORKING WITH FACES

Over time, after doing lots of faces, I have discovered my own shortcuts for certain facial features. Lining up facial details with your template will determine whether your portrait resembles the person or not.

PORTRAIT   10½" x 9½"

SIMILAR "SHORTCUTS"

If you examine the eyes and mouth of this face and the one in the example above it, you will see that they are done essentially the same way. You can practice doing faces using the pattern for this one on page 110.

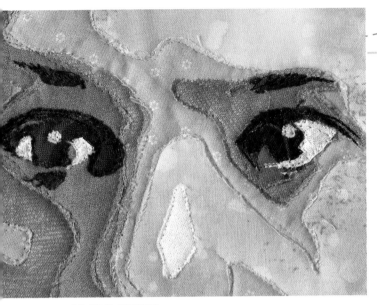

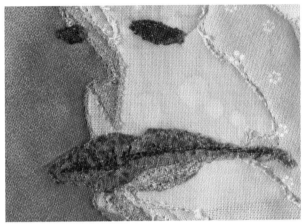

SIMPLE PIECES

A closer look at the eyes from PORTRAIT IN ORANGE on page 98 reveals that they are composed of very few, fairly simple pieces.

BASIC SHAPES

This close-up of the lips from PORTRAIT IN ORANGE on page 98 shows just how quick and easy a mouth can be. Choose one fabric for the mouth, use the back side of it for one spot of highlight on the lower lip and do the separation of the lips with thread.

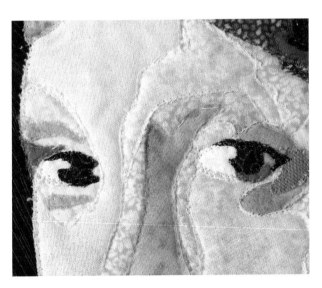

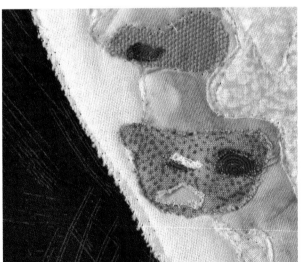

HIGH CONTRAST FABRIC (ABOVE)

The true drama of eyes comes from using high contrast fabric—white and black—and a white dot of light reflecting in each eye.

A BIT OF WHITE (RIGHT)

To depict lips that are slightly opened, just add a bit of white to indicate the teeth and a bit of dark fabric for the empty space. Otherwise, an open mouth is constructed the same way as a closed mouth.

Keep Leni's suggestion of a "little thread" in mind when creating faces. Don't overstitch. A wayward stitch can instantly change a facial expression. In this case, **less is best**!

NOTES FROM **NANCY**

99

ARTIST'S SHORTHANDS: LANDSCAPES

These shorthands will come in handy for landscape art quilts depicting elements of nature.

Water

An easy way to construct water using fabric is to begin with a base color and choose two or more additional colors whose value gets darker. I cut random and irregular strips and cut those into smaller pieces. Beginning near the shoreline (or in this case, the rocks), refer to the pattern only to see where the darker strips of fabric need to be placed. First, place the medium value followed by the darker value, especially near the base of the rocks. Fabrics with an interesting texture or pattern are more effective than solids, as they create more movement.

Rocks

If I tried to create rocks according to the pattern, I think I would go crazy! Instead, I use the pattern to establish where the darker areas and lighter areas should be. I cut fabric randomly, without measuring exactly to the pattern, but paying attention to those dark and light areas. These rocks were made with only four fabrics, plus just a small amount of the light fabric as the highlight. Remember that rocks are craggy, so don't cut perfect shapes; cut roughly and have fun with the process.

Trees

Because trees are so textural and each one is so different, it is not necessary to follow the pattern exactly. I focus on where the light, medium and dark values fall on the trees, and really only concentrate on the three main values and their placement. Trees provide an opportunity to have fun with fabric; lots of textures and unexpected prints make the trees more complex and interesting. Finishing with a free-flowing and random pattern of thread painting completes the picture.

Autumn Trees

When making a quilt of trees in autumn, I cut lots of random pieces of fabric, setting them onto the quilt using the patterns as a guide for placement. I do not worry about each individual piece, using the pattern mainly to tell me where the lighter areas, darker areas and negative space should be. Tree trunks and branches are done with the tracing, but not much else is. This is a very free-form and relaxing way to work on an art quilt. Using fusible web on the back of each fabric makes quick work of attaching everything when you are happy with the way it looks. Layer the quilt top onto batting alone and do a large stipple to hold everything in place.

WATER

Details like water let you break away from your pattern and experiment. Water can be impressionistic and still look great in your art quilt. Here, I used only a few fabrics: one as the base, a darker tone near the rocks and a lighter tone reflecting sunlight. (Detail from SEASCAPE, page 118.)

ROCKS

Rocks are fun to do; the key is to keep a variety of values in organic shapes. Think about your light source so that you highlight the areas of rock that would be reflecting sunlight. (Detail from ON THE ROCKS, page 36.)

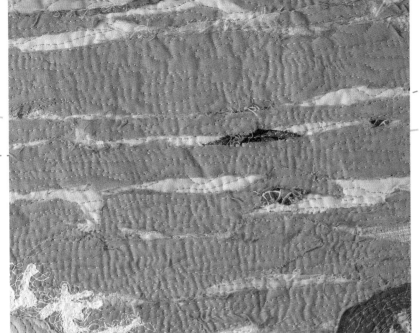

WATER AS BACKGROUND

When I started the water in ON THE ROCKS (pictured on page 36), I used a large number of blue printed fabrics in a variety of values. Some were quite unlike what one would expect to use for water. I cut little shapes and just put them together randomly. The end result was interesting, but much too distracting from the rest of the quilt, as the water was meant to be the background. Rather than do it again, I cut irregular strips of a lighter blue and laid them over the whole surface, allowing only little hints of the other colors to show through. It was "making lemonade," but it worked.

TREE TRUNKS

The key to making interesting trees is unexpected fabric choices. I love fabrics with writing on them, and they add a wonderful, whimsical texture to tree bark. Keep the roots looking natural by making their shapes very irregular, not straight across the base of the tree. (Detail from TREES IN A GROVE, page 118.)

AUTUMN TREES

AUTUMN (pictured on page 108) is all about color, and more specifically, orange and green. Pull together a wide assortment of greens and oranges (you only need small pieces), cut them randomly into small shapes and have fun placing them. Lots of unexpected patterns in these leaves are a nice surprise.

Chapter Six

PATTERNS AND PROJECTS

For many readers, you will be anxious to make your first art quilt of something that speaks to you and you feel compelled to create. For others, baby steps may be the way you want to approach this new world. This section contains your "baby steps." Some, like the pansy quilt, are easy and will serve as good practice for learning the process. Others are more challenging; and although they may seem daunting at first, as you become comfortable with making art quilts, they will seem less ambitious.

Many of the quilts I made specifically for this book are enclosed in this chapter along with the cutout pattern I used to create them. This will allow you to scan or copy the pattern to make it any size you want and use my finished quilt as a guide. But don't copy mine; use your own fabric stash, your own imagination and put your own stamp on it. I even gave these patterns fairly generic names so you wouldn't be influenced by MY vision.

You may want to copy the pattern in black and white so that you can comfortably change the colors in it. Fell free to make other changes to the pattern, crop it or add things to it. Go ahead: Let loose and have fun!

Even if you never plan to use any of these patterns for your own art quilts, look at them so you can understand what makes a workable pattern and how it is translated into fabric.

PANSY 16" x 16"

103

BLUE BOTTLE

Taken from a photo of a simple blue bottle, this quilt highlights the reflection of window light on the beautiful blue glass. The pattern is used as the specific step-by-step example in chapter three and is a great way to learn the process of creating a fabric collage. Remember, yours doesn't have to be blue—make it whatever color you want, just pay attention to value!

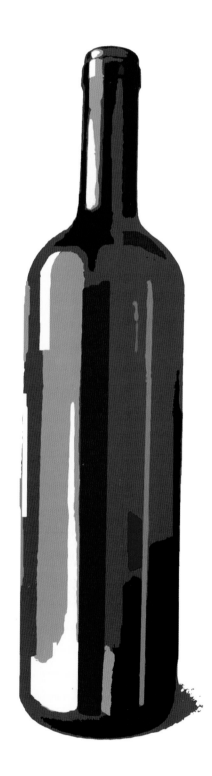

Blue Bottle 9" x 14"

PANSY

Pansy is probably the easiest quilt in the book to create, with a minimal number of pieces. My pansy is yellow and purple; yours can be any color you prefer. Think about using unexpected fabric patterns (look closely and you will see a purple fabric with writing on it) for a more outstanding art quilt.

NOTES FROM **NANCY**

Be certain to check out the DVD. Leni and I feature this quilt in great detail. It's an amazing process to see this art quilt unfold right before your eyes!

PANSY 16" × 16"

AUTUMN

I love autumn; the orange and reds of the changing leaves are favorite colors of mine. This pattern leaves a lot of room for you to play without following the pattern exactly. Focus on getting the tree trunks in the right place, then relax and have fun adding little bits and pieces of fabrics for your leaves. Instead of gluing each individual leaf piece, use fusible web on the backs of your leaves—you'll only have to press them to attach them! Use a variety of green fabrics.

NOTES FROM **NANCY**

Creating a nature art quilt is an ideal first project. Trees, blooms and landscape scenes are very forgiving since they don't include people or structures. Consider using this pattern to begin your photo-inspired art quilt venture.

Autumn 16" x 20"

PORTRAIT

Once you get started making art quilts, you will most likely prefer to make portrait quilts of people you know. This face will allow you to learn the basics; it was inspired by the beautiful face in Jan Vermeer's painting *Girl with a Pearl Earring*. Also check out the "artist's shorthand" for eyes and lips on page 98 for the easiest way to create details in portraits. The fabrics chosen for this quilt are discussed on page 52.

PORTRAIT 10½" × 9½"

FLAMINGOS

You may recognize this quilt from the discussion in on page 38 about combining photographs. This is the final result of looking at all the photos and using the elements from each that I thought were the strongest. I had a lot of fun choosing unexpected fabrics for the pink birds. This pattern is also a great way to practice working on water in an art quilt.

FLAMINGOS   15" x 14½"

SEASCAPE

SEASCAPE started as a photograph I took in one of my favorite places, Larchmont Harbor Park. The rocky shoreline is beautiful, and there are always a few sailboats around for the perfect seascape composition. The colors you use can completely change the mood of a quilt. If you make this quilt with softer, grayer blue fabrics, it will appear to be an overcast day; if you use brighter, more saturated blues, it will be a sunny day. Just remember that the farther in the distance, the lighter and grayer the fabrics should get. Check out the details for the thread-painted tree on page 76, the thread-painted appliqué sailboat on page 78 and the artist's shorthand for rocks and water on page 100.

SEASCAPE 19" × 16"

COLONNADE

Obviously, the columns in my original photograph were not purple, nor were the walls orange. But the quilt works because the values are correct. You can transform any photograph into a more dynamic art quilt by changing the colors, just as long as the values remain the same. This quilt is used as the example for elements that fall outside the quilt edge in exercise nineteen on page 91, but you can make it a rectangle quilt if you prefer. It's your artwork; you make the decisions.

NOTES FROM NANCY

The COLONNADE design is an ideal pattern to use color values from a different palette. Consider replacing the orange and purple colors of fabric with realistic shades or with other complementary colors that are across from each other on the color wheel.

COLONNADE 22" x 12"

TREES IN A GROVE

I decided to make this quilt in a monochromatic color scheme; primarily I used shades of green. I love the contrast of the tree trunks and the shadows. The horizontal format and the monochromatic colors make this scene restful and serene. Look closely to see how simply the trees are constructed, and read the notes for trees in the artist's shorthand on page 100.

TREES IN A GROVE   19½" x 15½"

TULIPS

I created this simple still life using a green glass vase that I've always loved. What would look more dynamic in a green vase than red or pink flowers? On page 32, we discussed that red is green's complementary color, and pink is a light value of red. Create your own still life compositions using your favorite items and combine them with fruit, flowers—whatever you want. Don't worry if your photo isn't perfect; it's only a guide.

TULIPS 13½" ×18"

LAWN CHAIRS

When I walk my dog, I always pass this house with Adirondack chairs on the front lawn. I love the shape of these chairs, which are actually bright blue. I took several photographs from different angles, combining chairs from two different photos. For a better composition, I chose to place the potted plant to add a spark of color between the two chairs. This scene always reminds me of lazy summer days. You may find this quilt a bit of a challenge, but if you take it one element at a time, it won't seem so hard.

LAWN CHAIRS   15½" × 19½"

ABOUT THE **AUTHOR**

Like so many girls of my generation, I first learned to sew in seventh grade Home Ec class. Although the skirt I made that semester could have been considered my initial foray into abstraction, I was hooked. My parents bought me my first sewing machine, which began a lifelong journey making everything from traditional quilts and clothes to home décor.

My entry into the world of art quilts began only a few years ago. It seemed a natural progression from my interests in sewing and photography. In 2001, I decided to change my life and began teaching traditional quilt classes. The following year, a business trip to the International Quilt Market in Houston for new class ideas introduced me to the amazing world of art quilts. Everything came together for me; I knew I had found my medium.

As a former photographer, I still see the world through the camera lens—captured moments in time: some poignant, some simply a brief glimpse into an unremarkable moment in the life of a stranger. It is my hope that viewers are drawn into my work in order to decide for themselves what the story is behind the image.

My work is shown in juried and invitational shows around the world, and I continue to teach both traditional and art quilting, as well as give workshops based on my first book, *Thread Painting* (Krause, 2007). I live and work at home in New Rochelle, New York, with my husband, Fred. My two sons, Jared and Jordan (whose childhood photos are often the subjects of my quilts), are now adults.

Please visit my Web site at www.leniwiener.com to see more of my work, a blog of new art quilts as they progress and information on classes and workshops.

RESOURCES

Your local quilt shop is the best place to find many of the products and materials recommended for use in this book. There are also many online sources; here are just a few:

WWW.LENIWIENER.COM
Visit the author's own Web site to purchase many of the items mentioned in this book and for information about workshops, classes and trunk shows of this book.

Computer Resources
Adobe Photoshop Elements free trial download:
WWW.ADOBE.COM

Free Web site to print enlargements for your patterns:
WWW.BLOCKPOSTERS.COM

Notions
Ruby Beholder
WWW.MARTINGALE-PUB.COM/STORE

Do-Sew
WWW.STRETCH-AND-SEW.COM

Nancy's Notions
WWW.NANCYSNOTIONS.COM

Superior Threads
WWW.SUPERIORTHREADS.COM

Books
Find more great quilting books at:
WWW.MYCRAFTIVITY.COM

To preview some of the newest fabric releases:

WWW.FREESPIRITFABRIC.COM
FreeSpirit Fabric

WWW.ROBERTKAUFMAN.COM
Robert Kaufman Fabrics

WWW.BLANKQUILTING.COM
Blank Fabric

WWW.PBTEX.COM
P&B Fabrics

INDEX

Adobe Photoshop, 13, 38
    filters, 44-45, 52
Appliqué, thread-painted, 74-75, 78-79
Artistic filter, photoediting, 44-45
Autumn, 100-101, 108-109

Background, 29-30, 67
    color, 62-63, 65
    water, 101
Backing, 84
Balloon Man Takes a Break, The, 29, 40
Batik fabric, 14, 51
Batting, 12-13, 78, 82-83
Binding edge, 84-89
Blue Bottle, 48, 65, 104-105
Borders, 80-83
Brushstroke filters, photoediting, 44-45

Camera, digital, 13
Challenge, 27
Collage, fabric. See Fabric collage, building a
Colonnade, 23, 116-117
Color
    background, 62-63, 65
    and mood, 50, 118
    solid, 14
    understanding, 32-33
Color saturation, 32-33, 50
Color scheme, monochromatic, 32, 120-121
Color temperature, 32-33, 50
Colors
    analogous, 32
    changing, 108-109
    complementary, 32-33, 62, 65, 108-109, 122-123
Composition, 114
    complex, 26
    one third/two thirds rule of, 21, 28-29, 37, 64-65
Computer, using a, 13, 16, 25
    See also Adobe Photoshop; Camera, digital
Conflicted Provenance, 31, 41
Contrast, 65
    facial, 98-99
Copyright, 22
Cropping
    people, 25
    photo, 19, 25
Cutout filter, photoediting, 44-45, 52

Darning foot, 12, 72
Depth, creating, 27
    See also Distance, depicting
Design, 16-17
Design, elements of, 19-33
    balance, 21
    color, 32-33
    composition, 19, 21, 26, 28, 114
    cropping, 19, 25, 35, 40-41
    eye, leading the, 21-22, 26-27, 29, 31, 36, 39
    format, 22
    framing, 27, 29, 39
    light, 30-31
    lines, 23, 26-27
    objects, number of, 28
    one third/two thirds rule of, 21, 28-29, 37, 64-65
    perspective, 24, 26
    shadow, 30-31
    snapshots, taking, 24
    story, telling a, 20, 29, 31, 36, 40
    subject, choosing a, 20
    visual weight, 29
Design, evaluating a, 16
Design wall, using a, 16-17
Details, using, 42-43, 69
    in patterns, 44
    thread-painted, 74-77
Distance, depicting, 27, 118-119
    with color, 32
    See also Depth, creating
Do-Sew, 13, 54

Edge finishes, 84-89
    binding, 84-87
    free-form shape, 85, 89, 91
    pillowcase, 84-85, 88, 91
Emotion, depicting, 20, 50, 90
Endless Dance of the Ponytail, The 40, 92-93
Eye, leading the, 21-22, 26-27, 29, 31, 36
    in photos, 39
Eyes, 98-99

Fabric
    attaching, 56-57
    buying, 14
    changing, 60
    choosing, 14-15, 49-51, 58, 116-117
    collecting, 12, 14-15

    cutting, 54-55
    hand-dyed, 14-15
    overlapping, 60-61
    printable, 78, 84
    sorting, 14-15
    storing, 15
    texture, 14, 50
    value, 3, 32-33, 50-51
    zinger, 33, 51
Fabric collage, building a, 9, 49-67, 69, 70
    background, 62-63, 65, 67
    complex, 66-67
    composition, 64-65
    fabric charting, 59
    fabric choice, 49-51, 58
    pieces, attaching, 56-57
    pieces, cutting, 54-55
    sewing together, 70
    values, 50-53, 58-60
Faces, 52-53, 98-99
    See also Portraits
Flamingos, 11, 112-113
Finishing, edge, 84-89
    binding, 84-87
    free-form shape, 85, 89, 91
    pillowcase, 84-85, 88, 91
Foamcore, 16-17
Focal point, 21-22, 24, 27, 41
Format, choosing a, 22
    horizontal, 22, 120-121
Frame, breaking free of the, 90-91, 108-109
Framing, compositional, 27, 29
    in photos, 39
Fusible web, 56-57, 100, 104

Glue, 56, 61

Headed Home, 23
Height, depicting, 22-23, 26, 28, 64
Highlights, 65
Horizon line, placing the, 21, 27, 64
Hue, 32-33

Inspiration, 19
Ironing, 55, 57

Jordan, 25, 43
Journal quilts, 97
Just Walk By, 70

Labels, 84
LADY ON THE TRAIN, 97
Landscapes, 21, 23, 27, 30, 32, 100-101
Leaves, 77, 101, 104-105
LAWN CHAIRS, 122-123
LIFE WAS SIMPLER WHEN ALL I NEEDED WAS TEDDY, 75
Light, 30-31, 51, 100
    overcast, 118-119
    overhead, 30
    side, 30, 65
    sun-, 118-119
LIGHTLY TOASTED, 18-19, 26, 95
Lines, 23, 64-65
    curved, 23
    diagonal, 23, 26-27, 64
    horizontal, 23, 26, 64
    vertical, 23, 64
Lips, 98-99

MARKET DAY, SARLAT, 68, 74
Mountains, 32
Mouth, 98-99
Movement, suggesting, 23, 90, 100
MUSEUM STEPS, 8, 75

Naming, quilt, 94-95
Nature, 104
Needles, sewing, 12
    selecting, 72

ON THE ROCKS, 36, 100-101
OUTSTRETCHED HAND, AN, 20, 75, 90

PANSY, 102-103, 106-107
PATIENCE, 41, 94
Patterns, 35-47, 60
    copying, 103
    creating, with a computer, 36-45
    creating, without a computer, 46-47
Perspective, 24, 26, 60
Photocopies, using, 46-47
Photoediting, 44-45
Photos, 9, 13, 66-67
    as color guides, 38
    combining, 30, 35-39, 112, 114
    and copyright, 22
    editing, 13 (see also Adobe Photoshop)

as inspiration, 19
organizing, 36
for pattern making, 35-47
versus snapshots, 19
    See also Snapshots
Pillowcase edge, 84-85, 88, 91
PINE BROOK, 22
PORTRAIT, 98, 110-111
PORTRAIT IN BLUE, 96
PORTRAIT IN GREEN, 50, 96
PORTRAIT IN ORANGE, 96, 98-99
PORTRAIT IN YELLOW, 96
Portraits, 50, 96, 98, 110-111
Puckering, preventing, 12, 76

Quilting, 84
Quilting foot, 12

Red viewer, 13, 50, 52
Reflections, 106-107
Rocks, 14, 100
Rod pockets, 84
Rotary cutter, 12

Scissors, 12, 54
SEASCAPE, 100, 114-115
Seascapes, 14, 23, 76-77, 118-119
Sewing machine, 12, 72-73
Shadow, depicting, 29-31, 51, 60
    with thread painting, 75
Signature, adding a, 94
Sizing, 16, 42-43
Skin tone, 15, 52-53
Snapshots
    cropping, 25, 35, 40-41
    evaluating, 38
    taking, 24
    versus photos, 19
    See also Photos
Software. See Adobe Photoshop
Space, negative, 21
Stairs, 26, 37, 81
Stitching, free-motion, 67, 72-73
Story, telling a, 20, 29, 31, 36, 40
Style, finding a, 9
    See also Voice, finding a
Subject, choosing a, 20

Supplies, 12-13
    binoculars, 16, 60
    embroidery hoop, 76
    freezer paper, 54-55, 57
    markers, 66
    pin cushions, 12-13
    pins, 12-13
    tracing paper, 54-55, 77
SUSPICION, 27

Templates, 54, 60
Texture
    fabric, 14, 50
    thread-painted, 69, 74
    tree, 24, 100-101
Thread, 12
    jump, 76-77
    selecting, 70-72
Thread painting, 9, 12, 67, 69-79
    appliqué, 74-75, 78-79
    attaching, 79
    direct, 74-77
    stitching, free-motion, 72-73
    thread for, 71
TOURIST SEASON, 22, 31, 34-35
Trees, 15, 76-77, 100-101, 104-105
    monochromatic, 120-121
    photographing, 24
    texture, 24
TREES IN THE GROVE, 101, 118-119
TULIPS, 120-121

Values
    color, 32-33, 108-109
    fabric, 32-33, 50-51
    facial, 52-53
    seeing, 13, 50-52
    understanding, 52-53
    using, 30-31, 108-109
Viewer, plastic. See Red viewer
Voice, finding a, 9, 20, 97
VOID, THE, 29

Water, 14-15, 100-101, 112-113
    photos of, 38-39
Weight, visual, 29

YELLOW HAT, 31

BRING MORE "ART" TO YOUR ART QUILTS!

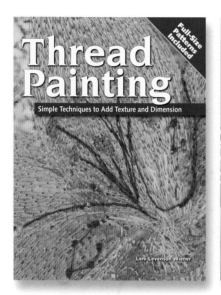

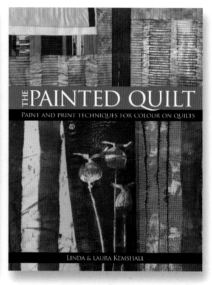

THREAD PAINTING

LENI LEVENSON WIENER

Use your sewing machine, computer and creativity to design stunning custom fabric art through thread painting. Identify various threads, tension and bobbins to use while you create 15+ projects, including totes, pillows and artwork for your home.

paperback; 8.25" × 10.875"; 128 pages
ISBN-10: 0-89689-435-5
ISBN-13: 978-0-89689-435-8
SRN: Z0379

SERGE AND MERGE QUILTS

SHARON V. ROTZ WITH NANCY ZIEMAN

Serging meets quilting in this title from the Create with Nancy series. Use your serger to both create and embellish 15 different quilt projects. Bonus DVD, hosted by Nancy Zieman, introduces and reviews the techniques found in the book. Break out your serger and get quilting!

paperback; 8.25" × 10.875"; 128 pages
ISBN-10: 0-89689-810-5
ISBN-13: 978-0-89689-810-3
SRN: Z2917

THE PAINTED QUILT

LINDA & LARA KEMPSHALL

Learn to color your cloth using a variety of techniques including fabric paints, pastels, dyes, bleaches and transfers. This book combines simple techniques to produce complex textile surfaces. Explore your own creative potential to achieve effective and original designs!

paperback; 8.25" × 10.875"; 128 pages
ISBN-10: 0-71532-450-0
ISBN-13: 978-0-71532-450-9
SRN: Z1347